Acting for Children

The Law Society's Handbook for Solicitors
and Guardians ad Litem Working with Children

*Incorporating Guidance from
the Family Law Committee*

by

Christine Liddle, *Guardian ad Litem*

Consultant Editors

Peter H F Jones, *Solicitor*
John Howell & Co

Michael Petley, *Solicitor*
Reader at The College of Law

*Both members of the Law Society's
Family Law Committee*

Illustrations by Willow

THE LAW SOCIETY

113 Chancery Lane
London WC2A 1PL

THRINGS & LONG

Acknowledgements

I would like to thank Ruth Lawrence, David Liddle,
Nigel Lowe, Clive Major, Carol Marks, Daphne Norbury
and Martha Street for all their encouragement and assistance
with this project. My thanks are also due to all those children,
including my own, from whom I have learned so much.

First published by

THE LAW SOCIETY

113 Chancery Lane
London WC2A 1PL

ISBN 1 85328 112 3
LS 7.5 (92)

Printed by Multiplex Medway Ltd,
Walderslade, Kent

Contents

Preface

This book is a prime example of what can be achieved by guardians ad litem and solicitors working together. Almost exactly eight years ago, in May 1984, section 103 of the Children Act 1975 was implemented to give courts power to appoint a guardian ad litem to safeguard the interests of children involved in court proceedings and thus began what is now generally regarded as a successful partnership between guardians and solicitors.

Coinciding with these developments the Law Society set up the Child Care (now Children) Panel and issued its first guidance to solicitors working with children and guardians ad litem. Practitioners have gained a lot of experience since those early days and the Children Act 1989 has, of course, changed the whole context in which proceedings are now conducted. Thus the Law Society's Family Law Committee has taken the opportunity of expanding and bringing up to date the guidance and this is set out in full at the end of the book. It is particularly appropriate that the guidance is published in a book written principally by a guardian in collaboration with solicitor members of the Family Law Committee as this really does show how much progress has been made in eight years in terms of solicitor awareness of the skills and working methods of guardians, and vice versa.

Talking recently to a German professor researching methods of representing children I learned that the German Ministry of Justice has some difficulty with the idea of social workers and solicitors working together. I was proud to report an English success story. This book is a testament to that success and deserves to be widely read as much for its guidance on practical problems as for its demonstration of how well the respective approaches of solicitor and guardian ad litem complement each other to provide a better form of representation for a child than either professional could provide acting alone.

Jane C Hern
Assistant Secretary-General
Co-ordination Division
The Law Society

Introduction

Working with children has assumed a new importance with the implementation of the Children Act 1989. It is significant that the principle that 'the child's welfare shall be the court's paramount consideration' is enshrined in the Act's opening paragraph, and that the 'ascertainable wishes and feelings of the child' is the first of a number of criteria to be considered by the court in making its decision. There has been extensive training and preparation of the judiciary, magistrates, lawyers, social workers and other professionals concerned with children in an unprecedented attempt to ensure the success of this radical reform of child care law.

The Law Society has for some time recognised the need for high professional standards in this field by maintaining a Children Panel of solicitors who are proficient and have proved their expertise in the specialist skills that are needed in child care work. The problem for solicitors wishing to specialise in this area is how to acquire the experience and necessary skills, and I hope this book may be of assistance in describing practical techniques and considerations that I have found helpful when working alongside legal colleagues with child clients. I write from the standpoint of a guardian ad litem working in public law cases, but I hope that most of what follows could equally well apply to children involved in divorce, where the solicitor may well be dealing with children without recourse to social work advice. Some of the practical suggestions may also be useful to barristers and other legal practitioners who work with children.

Lawyers are currently acutely aware of the constraints imposed by the requirement to be prudent with legal aid, and it is against this background that specialists in child care law are having to maintain the quality of their work. There are recommendations on the highest standards to be aimed for, but also recognition that the reality of what can be achieved with limited resources sometimes falls short of the ideal.

Working with vulnerable children can be demanding and painful, but is always interesting, and I hope this book will enable solicitors to gain confidence in using novel and unfamiliar methods to do the best for the children in their professional care.

Terms used in the text

There are of course practitioners of both sexes working as solicitors and guardians ad litem, but for the sake of clarity I have denoted the solicitor as male and the guardian as female. Similarly the child client is usually referred to as 'he' but my comments apply equally to girl children. 'Guardian' is a shortened version of 'guardian ad litem'.

References to 'the Act' are to the the Children Act 1989; references to 'the Rules' are to the Family Proceedings Courts (Children Act 1989) Rules 1991 (similar provisions are set out in the Family Proceedings Rules 1991).

Christine Liddle
July 1992

CHAPTER 1

Solicitors and guardians

Those solicitors and barristers who are used to practising in the adult courts with fellow lawyers as colleagues will find themselves in a quite different setting in the new Family Proceedings Courts, where most child care cases are heard in the first instance. The physical surroundings are likely to be more informal, with tables grouped in a small room rather than a dais for the magistrates and a witness box which may be intimidating for children and their families. The layout will vary from one court to another, but the drawing on page 110 suggests the most usual arrangement to be found at present. The clerk is likely to take a more prominent role, presiding over directions hearings in the absence of magistrates. Above all, the approach of all parties should be non-adversarial where possible, in recognition of the complex and sensitive issues in child care cases, which are often best resolved by agreement, or at least in a manner that does not further erode already fragile relationships.

The background to guardians ad litem

Lord Justice Butler-Sloss has described the guardian ad litem as the 'linchpin' of the whole system, and it may be helpful to describe in some detail the role of this individual. The title is obscure, to say the least, and unhelpful to families who may fear that this person becomes the child's guardian in the commonly accepted meaning of the word. In fact 'ad litem' means 'before the law' and allows the child, who has no legal personality, to be represented by an independent adult acting on his or her behalf. The guardian ad litem is only involved for the duration of the court proceedings, but plays a pivotal role during this period.

Prior to 1984, guardians ad litem were involved in adoption and some very limited child care matters. Following a number of highly publicised and tragic cases, including that of Jasmine Beckford, it was recognised that children's own wishes and needs should be given proper consideration by the courts, and that a social worker independent of the other parties (including the local authority) would help to promote the welfare of the child as the paramount consideration. The need to protect children from abuse within their own homes was a priority before 1987, when the events in Cleveland also highlighted the risks to children of misguided state intervention. The subsequent report prepared by Lord Justice Butler-Sloss went some way towards redressing the balance between children's rights and parental responsibility for their own children in such circumstances and it certainly contributed to and informed the current reform of the law concerning children. The independence of the guardian ad litem was recognised as an important element in maintaining the balance between protecting families from unwarranted local authority intervention and safeguarding children genuinely at risk. Guardians are acutely aware of the need to preserve their independence if they are to enjoy the confidence of the courts and the trust of parents, who can usually appreciate that the child's needs are the primary consideration.

Who are guardians ad litem?

Each local authority has the duty to maintain a panel of guardians ad litem, usually experienced and independent social workers, who are available for appointment by the courts. There have been variable arrangements in different parts of the country as to how these panels are operated. Some counties have a reciprocal arrangement with a neighbouring authority, where employed social workers undertake the guardian duties for a child in the other area. In other places, voluntary agencies such as Barnardo's or the Children's Society provide a guardian service on behalf of the local authority. The most common arrangement, however, is for authorities to use the services of self-employed, wholly independent individuals who work on a freelance basis, usually from their own homes. The local authority selects, supports and ultimately pays these guardians, but has to be scrupulous in not interfering in their professional work in order not to undermine their independence. This principle was upheld by judicial review of the attempt by Cornwall County Council to impose time-limits on its guardians (*R. v. Cornwall County Council ex parte Cornwall and Isles of Scilly Guardians ad litem and Reporting Officers Panel* (1991) 135 S.J. (L.B) 204. There is obviously a dilemma for local authorities in managing a service that is difficult to monitor, and it might well be preferable for guardians to be wholly independent of the local authority and independently funded to preserve their integrity in the eyes of the family, courts and other professionals. Despite the obvious drawbacks of the system as it operates at present, day-to-day practice seems to work, and in general the service has won recognition from the courts for the quality of its work in child care cases.

The appointment and duties of the guardian ad litem

Under section 41(1) of the Children Act, the onus is on the court to appoint a guardian ad litem on behalf of the child in a number of specified proceedings (section 41(6) and rule 10(1)) 'unless satisfied that it is not necessary to do so in order to safeguard his interests'. The specified proceedings include applications for a Care or Supervision Order, or the discharge or variation of such orders, Emergency Protection and Child Assessment Orders, and applications for Secure Accommodation Orders in non-criminal proceedings (rule 2(2)). Guardians also act in adoption cases, but have not usually instructed solicitors, although this may change now that adoption proceedings are 'family proceedings' for the purposes of section 8(3) of the Children Act.

The guardian ad litem is under a general duty under section 41(2) 'to safeguard the interests of the child', but more specifically under rule 11 he or she is required to appoint a solicitor to act on behalf of the child, to investigate all the circumstances of the case and prepare a report, and to advise the child appropriately over such matters as giving separate instructions to the solicitor or undergoing assessment or medical examination. Under rule 11(4) the guardian is also required to advise the court on such matters as who should be accorded party status (e.g. grandparents), timetabling of the case (to avoid delay which would be detrimental to the child), and the appropriate forum (which could lead to transfer sideways or upwards to another court). Transfer to a neighbouring court may be desirable if the case could be heard more quickly, or if several days' continuous hearing was required and could be provided there rather than locally. Another reason for transfer may be to consolidate proceedings, perhaps concerning other children of the same family, and transfer to a higher court may be sought by any party if the case is particularly complex or contentious.

The appointment and duties of the solicitor

The guardian normally appoints the solicitor to act for the child, unless the court has already done so, or the child himself, if he is sufficiently mature, has appointed his own solicitor. A parent or social worker would not be allowed to instruct a solicitor for the child because of the potential clash of interests. If there is a delay in the appointment of a guardian, the court may itself appoint a solicitor for the child, but the solicitor is then at a disadvantage in not having the advice of a guardian when taking instructions from the child at the first hearing (rule 12(1)(b) and (c).

Guardians would normally instruct a solicitor whose name is on the Law Society Children Panel, as some guarantee that he was suitably qualified to undertake this type of work. It is desirable to have a choice of solicitors working in a particular geographical area, so that the guardian may appoint the person most appropriate for a particular child. For example, a sexually abused girl may prefer a woman solicitor, or in a difficult case the guardian might select someone with good advocacy skills. Most guardians work with a number of solicitors, and learn from personal experience or the recommendations of their colleagues which are the best suited to the particular age group, sex or other characteristics of the child in question. There is a dilemma for guardians in 'trying out' solicitors who are new to the Panel, because no one wants to experiment when their child client's need for a good service may not be met, but they would also recognise that expertise in this field needs to become more widely available and untested solicitors have to be appointed to gain experience. A good way for solicitors to become established and known to guardians and to familiarise themselves with the workings of the Family Proceedings Court, is to act on behalf of parents and grandparents in the first instance. In the past, these clients have not always been well served by non-specialist solicitors, and ultimately children benefit if their families also feel they have been given a fair hearing. Solicitors beginning this type of work can also meet and learn from the experience of guardians and fellow legal practitioners by joining a local child care support group.

The solicitor's duty is to act on behalf of the child, but to take his instructions from the guardian ad litem unless the child is 'able, having regard to his understanding' to give his own instructions (rule 12(1)(a)). There are no clear guidelines as to when this threshold is crossed because children vary so much in their capabilities and development. A five-year-old child might have a strong opinion about who he wants to live with, but an imperfect understanding of the consequences of that decision. Similarly, a much older child might have learning difficulties and should not be expected to take responsibility for decisions about his future. The assessment of the child's ability to give separate instructions is something that must be discussed with the guardian, but ultimately the solicitor has to make up his own mind and act accordingly.

Working together

When the guidelines for solicitors and guardians to work in partnership were first drawn up, it was envisaged that the relationship between professionals from such different backgrounds was bound to be problematic. In fact, it has generally proved to be a fruitful partnership, and such difficulties as have arisen have been more between guardians and local authority social workers, who may feel their work is being duplicated or scrutinised.

It is important for the solicitor and guardian to meet or talk with each other early on in a case to sort out their mutual expectations, and to decide which one is to undertake the various tasks involved. The solicitor will want to complete the legal aid forms at the outset, and is likely to be the person who will accept delivery of documents on behalf of the child. As the case progresses, he should discuss with the guardian what written information should be disclosed to the child, and which one of them should do it. A solicitor would normally be under a duty to pass on all such information to an adult client, unless it could be harmful to him. In the case of children, the solicitor may need to withhold sensitive information such as a family illness, the illegitimacy of a sibling, or a criminal conviction of which the child is unaware. A 'mature' child may need to see all the information available before being able to give considered instructions to the solicitor, but a young child would not have the capacity to understand what is being presented to him. The solicitor needs to be sensitive to these issues when sharing written information with the child, and would be well advised to discuss with the guardian what should be disclosed and how it should be done.

Early on in the case the solicitor should be able to advise the guardian what the grounds for the application consist of, and he may need to liaise with the legal department of the local authority to get more details, and with the solicitors representing the child's parents to learn their reaction to the case. With the extensive documentation required of Social Services to initiate proceedings under the Children Act, it should now be clearer to all parties what the grounds are for the application, and how the local authority plans to implement the order it seeks. The guardian may need some initial legal advice about the actions of the local authority or, for instance, the desirability of seeking a transfer to a different court.

At this stage, the guardian will probably have an idea of the people she wants to interview and the documents she wishes to study, which will almost always include the Social Services file. The solicitor will want to avoid duplication, and would normally only re-interview parents, health visitors or teachers, etc., if he wants to call them as witnesses later on. The one person he will almost certainly wish to see is the child.

Seeing the child

Although children vary in their ability to give instructions, it is still very beneficial to the solicitor's understanding of the case for him to meet his child client, whatever the age. The Law Society and the Legal Aid Board accept that this is a reasonable requirement in the conduct of a child care case. Even a baby has his or her own characteristic personality, and a solicitor may learn much from the way the infant reacts with those about him, and the response he elicits from the person looking after him. It also helps the solicitor to have a clear mental image of his client throughout the proceedings: 'a child is a person, not an object of concern' (Lord Justice Butler-Sloss, in the Report of the Inquiry into Child Abuse in Cleveland, 1987).

An older child and the people looking after him will appreciate the personal interest of the solicitor, as a sign of the child's importance in the eyes of the court. He can explain the legal process in language appropriate to the child, and answer any questions or worries that the child or attendant adults may have, as the whole idea of the court is likely to be making them apprehensive. Getting to know the solicitor gives the process a human face and helps diminish their misgivings. As the solicitor gets to know the child he can weigh up the information being gathered by the guardian, as they work together to reach a final conclusion and recommendation to the court.

The older the child, the more direct work is likely to be undertaken by the solicitor, who may decide to take separate instructions if the young person is of sufficient understanding. There are very real difficulties in communicating with adolescents who may be monosyllabic or openly hostile, but their own wishes are likely to be given more weight by the court as they near maturity, and it is important that they are given proper legal advice and support as appropriate for young adults.

Working in partnership

Although the solicitor is likely to concentrate on the legal aspects, and the guardian on the social work issues of the case, there is a considerable degree of overlap as they attempt together to secure the best possible outcome for the child; their respective skills complement each other. The guardian usually works in isolation without the support of colleagues, and is likely to value her discussions with the solicitor as an opportunity to test out her ideas before coming to a firm conclusion. This sort of discussion can also be used as a 'dry run' for the issues that may come up subsequently in cross-examination. The solicitor may be able to suggest different legal remedies, and they may need to discuss the presentation of the child's case in court, including the use of witnesses apart from those being called by the local authority.

The use of expert witnesses

In discussion with the guardian, it might be decided to enlist the support of an expert witness on behalf of the child, either to challenge the evidence of another party or to give additional validity to a course of action proposed by the guardian. An example of the first kind of expert evidence might be in a case of ill-treatment, where the cause of a child's injuries might be in dispute. There are some little-known disorders whose symptoms might resemble non-accidental injury, or the reflex anal dilatation technique (which was much discussed by the Cleveland Inquiry) may be the basis of a case of possible sexual abuse. In either example a doctor specialising in that particular area of expertise may be able to assist the court.

The guardian may wish to use an expert witness to offer his assessment of a particular course of action.

Ryan and Tracey – should a brother and sister be placed separately?

Mr. and Mrs. Brown had two children, Ryan aged two, and baby Tracey who was three months old. The baby was sickly and after a hospital admission for failure to thrive, was found to have sustained many broken bones. A paediatrician stated that these injuries could not have been caused accidentally. The baby was discharged to the care of foster parents, and contact was maintained with her mother once a week. Ryan went to stay with relatives and saw his mother frequently. His father moved away, and the parents were eventually divorced.

Although both parents were questioned by the police, no evidence could be found as to who had caused the injuries and no prosecution was brought. The guardian considered that Ryan had a strong bond with his mother, but was less sure about the nature of the attachment between Tracey and her mother, and sought the views of an eminent child psychiatrist. He read all the documents, and saw both children with their mother on more than one occasion. His advice was that Mrs. Brown could probably meet the needs of one child, and that should be Ryan, with whom she had already established a good bond. The psychiatrist considered that the relationship between Tracey and her mother had been disrupted before it could be properly established, and that there was too much uncertainty surrounding the cause of her injuries for the risk to be taken in returning her to her mother. He recommended that she should be placed for adoption.

See also the example of Tina, in Chapter 4, page 46, for another case in which the evidence of an expert witness was invaluable.

The guardian should be advised that the agreement of the Legal Aid Board is needed in advance before any expert reports are commissioned, and the court should be asked for directions if the child is to be examined (rule 18(1)), or documents are to be disclosed to the expert (rule 14(2)(e)).

The temptation to use expert witnesses to add validity to a recommendation is strong, but there are a number of drawbacks. The Legal Aid Board has to approve the extra expenditure, and the availability of suitable practitioners is limited. The well-regarded experts are usually in great demand, and may not be able to see the child within a reasonable time span. The solicitor and guardian may decide the delay would be detrimental to the child, and that it would be preferable to go ahead without expert evidence.

Expert witnesses can usually be recommended by the guardian, her colleagues, other child care solicitors, or local hospitals and universities. The Law Society's Legal Practice Directorate Information Office also keeps an expert witness register.

Areas of possible conflict with the guardian

Working with children who have suffered neglect and cruelty can evoke strong emotions, and however professional the solicitor and guardian may be, there are occasions when they have sharply different perceptions of what is in the child's best interests. Many of these cases involve a degree of risk to the child, either of further injury if he returns home, or the emotional damage that can be caused by separation and the harmful effects of poorly resourced institutional care. The guardian's experience may give her more awareness of these hidden long-term risks, while the solicitor may attach more significance to the dangers of returning the child to inadequate parents.

Hopefully, further discussion should resolve these differences, but in the last resort rule 12(1) states that the solicitor must take instructions from the guardian, unless he believes the child to be of sufficient understanding to give separate instructions. In this case, the guardian should easily be able to accept that the child's wishes differ from her assessment of what is in his best interests, and that his right to have his point of view conveyed to the court by the solicitor should be respected. Rule 11(3)(b)(iii) now permits the guardian to be represented in her own right in these circumstances, but the local authority would have to meet her new solicitor's reasonable legal costs (regulation 9(1) of the Guardian ad Litem and Reporting Officers (Panel) Regulations 1991). In cases of continuing conflict, the guardian may apply for the solicitor's appointment to be terminated, but must give reasons, and the solicitor can make representations. There is no explicit provision for the solicitor to have the appointment of the guardian terminated, but in the last resort if he really could not work with her, he could seek the directions of the court who can terminate the guardian's appointment under rule 10(10) or resign his appointment, though that is rarely likely to be in the best interests of the child.

CHAPTER 2

Meeting the child

Working with children as clients demands a completely different approach from that used with adults. Normally a solicitor would expect to offer an initial appointment in his office, assess the client's legal problem, offer advice and take instructions, all in a fairly short interview. He or she would be wearing dark formal clothes, would sit behind a desk, and be able to maintain a physical and mental distance from the client, enhanced by the trappings of his office.

To work with children, a solicitor or guardian must be willing to engage with them personally, while not losing sight of professional obligations. The thought of dealing with distressed or antagonistic children can be very threatening for adults who are uncomfortable in unstructured settings with an unpredictable outcome. People with children of their own may feel that they are used to talking to and playing with little ones, but it can be misleading to compare child clients with one's own children. They will probably have experienced more damaging or deprived circumstances which will have adversely affected their development, so it may be necessary to revise one's opinion of what is 'normal' for a particular child. In addition, one's role as a parent involves 'managing' the child, but a responsible solicitor must respect his child client's autonomy, and not unconsciously manipulate him or her towards a particular course of action.

An advantage of being a parent or having regular contact with young relatives is that the solicitor is less likely to feel inhibited or embarrassed in dealing with children, and will probably know what current pop groups or latest fads are in fashion. The most important mental attitude is to feel comfortable with whatever approach is chosen, and to allow plenty of time to go at the child's pace.

Timing of work with children

With the pressure of other work, and the need to watch costs, it may be difficult for a solicitor to justify the amount of time needed for child care cases, especially in the present climate of financial constraints. There may well be travelling involved, if the child is in a foster home or with relatives some way away, and ideally the solicitor should allow for several meetings before he can be sure of the child's response. It could be completely counter-productive to seek to take instructions as he would from an adult client; he should aim, instead, to get to know the child gradually, observe his reactions, and only when the relationship is comfortable, should he try to gain more positive answers to how he is to represent the child's wishes in court. These aims can usually only be achieved over several meetings, and should never he rushed, though of course emergency applications require a different approach and are discussed below. At a first meeting, a solicitor should normally only expect to introduce himself, and start to relate to the child, to build the foundations for more substantial work later on.

The timing of work is significant, especially taking into account the child's age and cognitive development. The younger the child the shorter his concentration and memory span, so more is likely to be achieved in several short visits at frequent intervals. An older child can retain more information from one visit to the next, and may be able to discuss several issues at a time, but if more than a fortnight elapses between one interview and the next, the solicitor will have to repeat most of what was previously dealt with before he can move on. Sometimes it is inevitable that several weeks go by between interviews, because of holidays, or if a young person is in secure accommodation a long way away, but the working relationship between child and solicitor is likely to be less effective if this is the case.

Choosing a venue for the first meeting

In ideal circumstances, a solicitor would discuss in advance with the guardian what would be the most appropriate setting for his first meeting with the child, and who else ought to be present. Hopefully the child will already have met the guardian, who would be the obvious person to make the introductions. It is important to choose a place where the child feels comfortable, and that is unlikely to be the solicitor's office, although an older child may have experienced visiting other professionals such as a child psychiatrist in a formal setting, and could cope with this environment. More usually the best place to choose will be the foster home or children's home if the child is in residential care, or it might be at his school, a social services office or some 'neutral' venue like a cafe or park. The advantage of seeing a child in his foster home is that he is in a familiar place, and the solicitor can also learn from the foster mother how the child is settling in. The drawback is that the child may feel inhibited from expressing his real view about his home for fear of upsetting or offending his foster parents. A school can be a good choice, as long as the child does not feel stigmatised or embarrassed. It is the child's own territory, and offers opportunities for getting to know the child gradually, while walking around rather than being 'trapped' together in a small room. It is obviously necessary to have the permission of the head teacher and to choose a time that is least disruptive to the child's school timetable.

There can be difficulties in arranging to see a child who is still living in his own home, because of the need to talk to him privately, and because it is difficult for him to talk freely about his parents when they may be hovering nearby. Home visits are best avoided in these circumstances, but if there is no choice, the solicitor could still suggest taking the dog for a walk, or going to the local shops on some errand. Guardians and solicitors need to be flexible and fast thinking—one of my most productive interviews was conducted behind a hedge while out blackberrying with a child. He found it difficult to express his feelings, and was more comfortable if I could not see his face while he was talking. Similarly, car journeys release the child from a face-to-

13

face interview which is likely to make them clam up, though this is not likely to be an appropriate choice for a first meeting.

Dress

What the solicitor wears may affect his relationship with the child. If the interview takes place during a busy working day it may be inevitable that he or she is dressed for court, and some older children might prefer their 'brief' to look the part. Little ones might be intimidated by a looming figure in a dark suit, and judges now routinely remove their wigs if seeing young children. A solicitor should be prepared to get down to ground level both literally and metaphorically with young children, so comfortable, washable clothing is to be preferred, though anything too scruffy or informal may not impress the foster mother!

Meeting a child for the first time in court

Sometimes it is unavoidable for the first meeting to take place in court, if, for example, the solicitor has just been appointed, or the proceedings are of an emergency nature. There are very real problems in these circumstances, because the solicitor might need to make a fast assessment in order to support or oppose an application on behalf of the child, while the child is likely to be distressed, frightened or bewildered by the events that have brought him to this building. A newly appointed guardian might have similar difficulties and not be able to give clear instructions. In this case, the solicitor might ask for a quick return to court when he and the guardian will have been able to make a preliminary assessment of the child's needs.

From the child's point of view, the solicitor is likely to be just one of a number of strange people he will encounter that day, and unless there is something remarkable about his personal appearance, or some activity or event that stands out in the child's mind, he may well have forgotten him by the next time they meet. Introductions and explanations should be kept very simple, along the lines of, 'Hallo, John. My name is Bill and I'm your solicitor. I work in the court. Mary (the guardian) and I will be getting to know you over the next few weeks, so that we can tell the people in the court how you're getting on, and what you think about what's happened'. It is a good idea to give the child a piece of paper with your name and telephone number on so that he can contact you independently—see the suggested format on page 109. This explanation will subsequently need to be repeated and refined, with the difference between the respective roles of the solicitor and the guardian explained in due course, and the possibility of separate instructions canvassed if it becomes appropriate.

Waiting

There is often a lot of hanging about in courts, and the solicitor can begin to get to know the child during this waiting time. If the child is very distressed, he or she may just want to be cuddled or reassured by a familiar person, and it is unlikely that any child will be able to concentrate for long in these circumstances. I carry some simple games, puzzles and small soft toys in my brief case to entertain children while they are waiting, and pencil and paper games like 'hangman' or 'battle-ships' can be used with older ones. Electronic toys are popular but likely to irritate bystanders. Just sharing some sweets, or getting the child a drink can help tremendously, and all these activities provide a 'hook' for subsequent work. One child expected me to always have the same kind of peppermints when I saw him, because they had been a source of comfort on the traumatic occasion when we first met. Another child liked to play cards with her solicitor while they talked, because this was what they had done in the court waiting room.

One positive aspect of seeing a child for the first time in the 'crisis setting' of court, is being able to observe the reactions of his parents or other adults in this stressful environment, before their behaviour and emotions become more controlled and also to see the mutual response of the child and his family. The solicitor can get the feel of the case, and form first impressions of who is important to the child. Sometimes a lack of distress, or over-readiness to talk to unfamiliar people can in itself be a worrying symptom of superficial emotional behaviour.

Talking to children and explaining your role

Solicitors who are more used to adult clients may wonder how to start a conversation with a child. A useful jumping-off point is to start 'where the child is', rather than trying to impose one's own agenda at the outset. A positive comment about what the child is wearing: 'I like your red shoes, are they new?', or, 'What's your teddy's name?' can break the ice, and show that you are interested in the child's own interests. A young child may identify you as a friend of the social worker or foster mother, and a more sophisticated explanation would not be possible. Older children can be told that your work is in the courts, and that solicitors are trained to talk to judges and magistrates on behalf of their clients, so that they do not have to speak for themselves. Solicitors who meet children in the court building can more easily be identified in the child's mind with the legal process, but the Children Act specifies circumstances in which children should not attend court (rule 16). The presumption under previous legislation was that children would attend unless specifically excused, and now the opposite is true. It may therefore be more difficult to explain the role of the solicitor if meeting the child away from the actual court building. Most children, however, will have seen solicitors, barristers and judges on television, and have some idea, not always very accurate, that can be built on. A useful way of distinguishing between the role of the guardian and solicitor, is for the former to say something along the lines of, 'My job is to listen to what you say, tell that to the court, and also to tell the court what I think would be best for you'. The solicitor can say to a mature child, 'My job is to tell the court what you want me to say to them', or to a younger one, 'I am your helper in court'. Both should help the child to understand that the judge or magistrates ultimately decide what should happen, and that the responsibility belongs to those adults rather than the child himself.

Uncommunicative children

Talking to non-verbal, inarticulate or hostile children can be heavy going, but the child needs to be engaged somehow in a dialogue. The solicitor may find himself doing most of the talking, with only grunts or shrugs to indicate how the child feels about what is being said. As a last resort the solicitor may have to outline what he thinks has happened, and hazard a guess what the child thinks about it, 'I know you find it hard to say that you want to live with your dad, because your mum will be upset, but that is what I'm going to tell the court, OK?' He must then observe the child's body language very carefully to see if he is reading the child's feelings correctly, and be prepared to alter his statement and try again, until he gets a more positive response. It is of course most unwise to ask leading questions of a vulnerable child who may be used to placating adults, and will give the answer he thinks is required. It is helpful, in these circumstances, to ask the guardian if she has found a method of evoking a response, or has had similar difficulties. In extreme cases, it might be necessary to inform the court that it has proved impossible to gauge the child's wishes.

Occasionally a child may react strongly against seeing a guardian or solicitor at all.

Sharon—a child who would not talk

Sharon, aged 10, was an emotionally very disturbed child who had come into care following an allegation of sexual abuse by her father. She found the initial court appearance, medical examination and police interviews highly traumatic. She first met the guardian at court, but clung to the teacher who was accompanying her, and resisted any attempt to engage her in conversation. When the guardian later visited her at the special school, Sharon was brought into the room by her teacher, and became extremely agitated and fearful, screaming at the guardian and backing away from her. After taking advice from the teacher, the guardian sat quietly in the classroom observing Sharon, but did not persist with a direct interview. She had to base her report on the interpretation by Sharon's foster parents and teacher of her wishes rather than being able to talk with the child herself, which could have further damaged an already very vulnerable young girl.

Adolescents are notoriously moody, and if the solicitor has children of his own in this age group he may quickly become exasperated at what he sees as typical rebellious behaviour. Teenagers might well be intrinsically anti-authority, and however well-meaning the solicitor, he is likely to be seen as someone else just trying to hassle the youngster. As well as the usual problems of trying to communicate with young people in this age group, a girl or boy who has been abused may be especially confused or embarrassed at discussing their feelings and wishes with the solicitor.

Carol—a hostile young client

Carol, aged 14, came from a large rural family, well known in the area for their spectacular feuds and criminal activities. She alleged that an uncle had sexually abused her and was placed with foster parents. The first time she met the guardian in the foster home she responded well to her interest, and said she was frightened of meeting her parents in the court the next day.

The following day, the guardian introduced Carol to the solicitor, who arranged for her to wait in a different room from her parents.

They were extremely angry, and accused their daughter of telling lies.

Several weeks later, Carol wanted to return home, saying she had been lying, although the social worker thought some abuse had in fact occurred. Carol was extremely abusive to the guardian, and on a separate occasion to the solicitor, refusing to explain herself, and swearing effusively. This response was partly learnt from her family who were accustomed to dealing with authority in this way, but also served to cover her embarrassment for apparently changing her mind and putting everyone to a lot of trouble. The guardian and solicitor recommended to the court that she should go home, in accordance with her stated wishes, but also acknowledged that Carol's homesickness might render her vulnerable to abuse in the future, and suggested a number of safeguards to monitor the situation.

Children's language

One of the pitfalls of working with children is 'talking down' to them, which will result in a lack of trust and respect for the adult concerned. On the other hand, the solicitor must be able to express ideas and questions in simple words that are familiar to the child. He will need to find out from the child's caretaker or guardian what words the child uses to describe his parents, grandparents or other significant people, and the child's own interpretations of events. Adults may struggle to express painful and difficult truths in anodyne language, when children can often state the same idea with brilliant simplicity.

James—a child's view of events

James, aged five, had experienced a chaotic early childhood with his young mother. After many upheavals he had been placed for adoption, and his new parents were wondering how to help him make sense of his past. James had his own explanation which would suffice until he was old enough to understand a more complex interpretation. He said to them one day, 'My mummy didn't know how to look after children, so I came to live with you instead'.

It is necessary to be cautious in the interpretation of children's language. Inarticulate speech or dialect can lead to misunderstanding. A child once told me that his mother could not look after him 'because she was bad'. At first I was concerned that he should have acquired such a negative view of his mother, until I realised that 'bad' was his word for 'ill'. A child whose first language is not English may need to be interviewed with the assistance of someone he trusts, such as a teacher, who could act as an interpreter.

Fantastic statements by the child may appear as lies, when really they represent the child's partial understanding of what has happened to him, or his desire to try and control events that otherwise are incomprehensible.

Jason—lies, fantasies or partial truth?

Jason, aged four, had been rejected by his long-standing foster parents because they found his sexualised behaviour unacceptable. They delivered him without warning to another home found by the social worker. Jason told his new foster mother, 'I took Daddy's car and drove here because he was being naughty. I kicked him so he went away'. The real reasons for such drastic adult disapproval were a mystery to him, and he needed to make his own sense of what had happened, so as not to feel completely powerless.

Continuity of interviews

Children's memories and sense of time are much shorter than those of adults, and the significance they attribute to people or events are likely to be much more selective. Adults are sometimes shocked by children's apparently matter-of-fact acceptance of the death of a near relative, and their curiosity about what happens to the body, which can seem callous and misplaced. Children are more likely to be interested in day-to-day events—what's on TV tonight, who is going to buy me new football boots—than the outcome of a far-off court case. That is not to say that children are not affected by uncertainty, because their concentration and ability to learn satisfactorily in school can certainly be impaired if they are feeling insecure. It is rather that they cannot hold anxieties at the front of their mind in the same way as adults.

It is necessary, therefore, to go over the same ground at the beginning of each interview, and try to establish what the child has remembered and understood. The solicitor will need to remind the child of his name, his job, his relationship to the guardian, and what he will say on behalf of the child in court as that becomes clearer. It is useful to have some means of linking one interview with the next in the child's perception. This might mean dressing in a similar way (wearing the same brooch or tie), bringing the same toys each time, or saying, 'Do you remember when you saw me last time, Mrs. Jones brought you here in her blue car, and we went to feed the ducks?' It is not always necessary to see the child in the same place, and indeed it is preferable to see how he reacts to different people in different settings. The guardian may want to attend contact visits between a child and his mother, or see how he relates to other children at a nursery, and the solicitor may find some occasions are more productive than others.

Kathy — a useful car journey

Kathy was a 15-year-old girl living in a children's home the other side of town from her mother. Her stepfather was remanded in prison accused of raping her, but her mother was torn between her loyalties to her husband and daughter. Kathy's solicitor met her in court, and at the children's home, but only got monosyllabic replies from an obviously very unhappy young woman. The contact between mother and daughter was difficult to maintain because of the poor bus service between the children's home and the estate where Kathy lived. The solicitor offered Kathy a lift to her home, and found her much more talkative in the car. Kathy appreciated the solicitor's kindness, and began to trust her with her fears and mixed feelings about the situation in which she found herself.

A male solicitor might need to be more cautious in this sort of situation. Children who have been sexually abused can misinterpret innocent gestures of friendship, and it would not be helpful to the child or solicitor to be alone in a car together. Children and young people who have been abused and neglected know how to inflict damage on themselves and others, as if to confirm in their own eyes that they are worthless. This destructive behaviour is seen most often in young people where a secure accommodation order is sought.

Confidentiality

Solicitors working with adult clients have a duty of confidentiality, and the child client is entitled to the same care, but there may be exceptional circumstances where the solicitor's duty to act in the child's best interests override the duty of confidentiality. The most difficult problem to arise in this area would be if the child disclosed sexual abuse or a serious criminal offence concerning a third party and did not want the solicitor to tell anyone else. The Law Society guidance on this issue suggests that the solicitor should try and persuade the child to reveal the abuse, but if he is unsuccessful he should consult the guardian, who could then take the appropriate steps to protect the child. If there was no guardian available, the solicitor may in the final analysis decide that the child's welfare takes precedence over the duty of confidentiality and refer the matter to the police or social services.

In cases where the guardian and solicitor had parted company, and the latter was taking instructions directly from the child, it would no longer be appropriate for the lawyer to disclose to the guardian any matter that the child wanted kept confidential, except in the circumstances outlined above.

Building a good working relationship with the child client

Children are most likely to communicate their wishes effectively if they feel safe and comfortable with the solicitor, and this may only emerge on the third or fourth occasion. A child may need to test out how reliable and trustworthy this person is before he can confide his real feelings, and it is vital that the solicitor *is* reliable, and does what he says he will do. It is no good making an appointment that cannot be kept, or promising to give a message that is then forgotten. The solicitor must keep to agreements and be punctual with his child clients, and devote enough time to go at their pace, if he is to be successful in this kind of work.

CHAPTER 3

Working with children

Having talked to the guardian about respective tasks concerning the child, and probably having met the child client for the first time, the solicitor should now be thinking of what he wants to achieve in his direct work with the child. There are three main objectives:

(1) to observe the child, and compare impressions with those of the guardian in the light of information being gathered from other sources (family members, teachers, social workers, etc.);

(2) to help the child understand the court process, and the different options available; and

(3) to elicit the child's own wishes and feelings about his future, and to decide whether or not he is capable of giving separate instructions.

These three tasks will probably coincide and overlap, and the time needed will vary from child to child. The solicitor will need to see an older child more than once, but even a baby should normally be seen on at least one occasion. He will not be able to express himself directly, but observation of the way he responds to his caretakers, and objective data such as patterns of eating, sleeping and growth will give some indication of his well-being or otherwise. Information about the court process and the meaning of different orders available will be helpful to his foster parents, or parents if their own solicitor has not explained the situation to them adequately. People often need to hear the same information several times before it is really grasped, especially if their understanding is impaired by anxiety, or they have learning difficulties.

Observation of the child

This can best be carried out in a relaxed setting where the child is comfortable, although as previously noted, much can also be learnt from a child's behaviour in the court. The guardian will probably want to see the child in a number of different circumstances—in the foster home, the classroom, and on a contact visit with his parents. The solicitor should not duplicate such visits, but can discuss the guardian's observations with her and compare them with his own. He may be an amateur in contrast to the guardian, who is supposed to be an expert with children, but his views are still useful. The magistrates are lay people, and it can be helpful to the guardian to test her perceptions of the child with someone who is not so closely involved.

To create a relaxed atmosphere with a child, it is important not to be rushed, and to find an enjoyable activity with which to start one's work with the child. The solicitor might take some toys, drawing materials or storybooks with him, or use something available in the home. I once arranged to meet a solicitor at the foster home of a 10-year-old girl. While we were waiting, Kim showed me her collection of marbles, which provided a lively three-sided game when he arrived. It also had the advantage of getting him down on the floor, to scrabble under the sofa for lost marbles, making him much more approachable for this particular child.

If a solicitor is meeting a child in school it can be helpful to ask him or her to take him on a guided tour. He will learn what subjects the child enjoys or not, his general feelings about the school and his teachers, how he gets there, what sort of lunch he has, and also the reaction of other pupils as they walk around. He will begin to form an impression of the child's intelligence and ability to express himself.

A shared activity such as doing a jigsaw puzzle, playing a game or looking at a storybook are all good ways of breaking the ice. Older children can be asked about their favourite pop groups or football teams, and TV programmes they like to watch. Accompanying a foster mother to meet a young child from school, or taking a youngster to the swings (probably with a familiar adult the first time), all provide a means of getting to know the child in an unforced manner before engaging in more focused work.

Helping the child to understand the court process, and different outcomes

The solicitor's role of advising the child about the legal process is an important one, best carried out by someone immersed in the law rather than the guardian or social worker whose knowledge is more partial. The solicitor must always remember that his child client has a limited understanding, and must simplify his language and explanations accordingly.

It is easier to explain the court building and personnel to children who have attended, but this is becoming less common under the provisions of the Children Act. The solicitor might have to rely on drawings (freehand or using the one on page 110), or build on what the child already knows about the law (people wearing funny wigs or being sent to prison). He can explain the likely length of the proceedings using a calendar or diary, and any current issues such as directions about contact, medical examinations or bail conditions.

Hannah—explaining the significance of an order

Hannah's parents were facing serious criminal charges arising out of their alleged ill-treatment of her little brother. Hannah's statement to the police was likely to form an important plank of the prosecution case. Her parents were bailed on condition that they did not attempt to contact Hannah. She felt guilty that what she had said had got her parents into trouble, and fearful of their reaction when she did see them next.

The solicitor helped Hannah to cope with these feelings by explaining that the court had ordered that there should be no contact for a limited period, so that she could not see them even if she had wanted to.

This case is a good example of the conflicts that can arise between the needs of the prosecution and good child care. While the police did not want their evidence contaminated, Hannah needed help in resolving her relationship with her parents. Eventually the solicitor representing Hannah was able to persuade the police to modify the bail conditions to allow an exchange of letters, and this first step enabled the social worker to help Hannah and her parents work through what had occurred without compromising the subsequent trial.

Explaining the different sorts of orders has become more complex with the advent of the Children Act. There are now more to choose from than simply a Care Order or Supervision Order, and there can be different permutations and time scales. Except for much older or unusually competent children, it is probably too difficult to understand the whole range of orders available. The child himself will chiefly be concerned about where he is to live, and who he can see, as well as how important decisions about his future will be made. At the beginning of his work with the child, the solicitor is probably best able to explain the range of different orders by saying that the court can choose different ways of deciding what is best for the child. As the solicitor and guardian firm up their final recommendation, the solicitor can then explain in more detail to the child the legal implications of the chosen order. A solicitor who accepts separate instructions from an older child will have more of a responsibility to explain the choices available, and what the different consequences might be. He can explain the general duty of confidentiality and, if appropriate, the circumstances where he might have to share information with other professional people.

As with all information given to children, these legal explanations will need to be repeated several times, both in simple language and maybe written or diagrammatic form. It is also worth ensuring that the child's caretakers understand the legal aspects so that they can answer his questions or reinforce the information given between visits. Children do not always ask the right person at the right time what they want to know, and it is important for a foster mother to be equipped to reassure a child who is lying awake worrying about an impending hearing.

Discovering the child's own wishes and feelings

The guardian will need to be satisfied that she and the solicitor understand what the child wants, so that they can conscientiously represent his views in court. The guardian may have to tell the court that these wishes do not coincide with recommendations of her own. The solicitor has a duty to relay an older child's wishes without qualification, but only if he has decided that the child is mature enough to give him separate instructions—otherwise he has to follow the guardian's instructions.

Most guardians have developed their own methods of communicating with children, and have experience about what works well with different age groups or abilities. It may be helpful to describe in some detail the techniques that I use, and the equipment I usually take with me. Babies can be engaged with rattling car keys, or the contents of a handbag, but children from three or four upwards to about 10 are more likely to respond to the contents of my toy kit, which is carried in what I hope is an intriguing bag with an elephant on the front.

My toy kit

I change the contents of my toy bag from time to time but at present it consists of:

two soft glove puppets;

a set of nesting Russian dolls;

a squeaky nursery toy;

a set of four Duplo houses (Duplo is a chunky, baby version of Lego);

Duplo people, animals, cars and furniture;

a toy telephone;

a miniature kaleidoscope;

an animal mask;

simple story books;

a set of felt-tips, pencils and drawing paper.

I usually let the child tip the contents out onto the floor, and play with whatever takes their fancy. Some of the items are purely for fun, while others can be used to talk with children indirectly about their feelings. The puppets can 'talk' to each other, or the child may feel safer behind the mask to speak about frightening or unsafe topics. The Russian dolls are useful for talking about families, especially babies and mothers, and are a good test of children's manual dexterity and memory (putting them back together in the right order). The toy telephone can be used to find out children's feelings about absent parents.

Cindy—using toys to release feelings

Cindy, aged 10, and her younger brother came into care after the latest episode of their mother's mental illness. They were very attached to her, but frightened and bewildered by her bizarre behaviour. They were in a foster home that discouraged contact with natural parents, and I thought it was more likely that Cindy would express her real feelings about her mother in a different environment. I arranged to see her in school, but when I arrived the only room available was the secretary's office, with the secretary in it!

After playing for some time with the toys, Cindy became less conscious of the presence of the secretary and myself. She picked up the toy telephone, and I asked who she would like to talk to. I pretended to use the real telephone, and talked to her as if I were her mother. Cindy became very tearful, and wanted to know why her mother had not visited her, and angry that she had broken her promise not to do 'naughty things' in public.

This conversation seemed to release many of Cindy's pent-up feelings and enabled me to better understand her ambivalence towards her mother, although I subsequently had to reassure the secretary who had been upset herself at the intensity of Cindy's distress. There is a fine balance to be maintained between acknowledging and accepting the pain the child is experiencing, but not adding to it unnecessarily. The adult attempting to help the child should not gloss over uncomfortable subjects in order to save their own feelings of discomfort or embarrassment.

The toy houses and people are also very useful in talking about families and places where the child has lived. Children quite readily identify the different figures with people they know, and can enter into the spirit of pretend games as long as the adult does not feel too silly. I might start by asking the child which figure looks like him, and describing with appropriate actions and toy cars how the social worker brought him to live with Auntie Mary and Uncle Bill, what furniture he has in his room, where the dog sleeps, etc., etc. Then we might describe the people left at home, and how the social worker might bring one of them to see him. The child usually gets quite absorbed in these games, and by using the same figures and remembering who is who, different themes can be explored in successive visits.

Jamie — using toy people

Jamie, aged four, liked playing with the toys but could not concentrate for very long. His passion was for cars, and he enjoyed zooming up and down the room with them. He was in care because of suspected abuse by his mother's boyfriend.

Jamie eventually settled down to playing with the houses and toy people. We identified different members of his family. When he had picked out a toy person to be his mother's boyfriend, Jamie became very aggressive and threw the figure down behind a radiator. I attempted to retrieve this figure, saying he belonged with the others, but Jamie shouted, 'No, no, I don't want him'—a clear indication to me of his fear and dislike of this man.

Guardians and solicitors are not qualified to offer psychological interpretations of children's play, but an incident such as this could be described to the court as part of the overall attempt to convey a young child's wishes.

Drawing

With children from eight or nine upwards I find that drawing, both freehand or using outlines such as those on pages 108–112, can be very successful. I might start by drawing an outline of a square house and asking the child to describe who lives in it. There is generally great amusement at my defective drawing skills, but it helps me to sort out the names, ages and relationships of different family members, including the pets. There might have to be a number of houses to include the child's own home, his foster home, nan and grandad, etc. One child was helped by drawing a prison with his abuser firmly locked up in it.

These portraits of people significant to the child can be used in a subsequent interview to try and tease out his feelings towards the different members, as in Peter's picture.

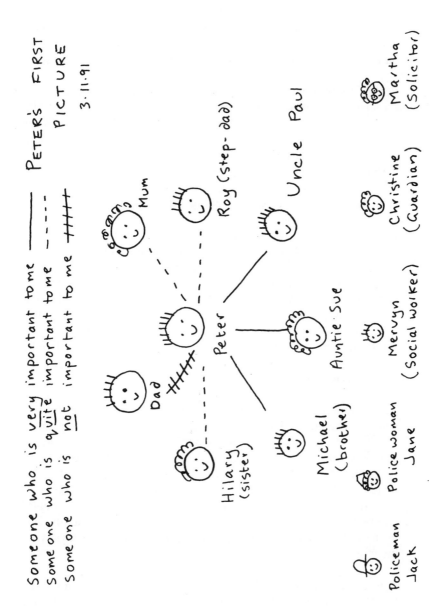

Someone who is very important to me ———
Some one who is quite important to me - - - -
Some one who is not important to me ++++++

PETER'S FIRST
PICTURE
3.11.91

Mum
Roy (step-dad)
Uncle Paul
Dad
Peter
Auntie Sue
Hilary (sister)
Michael (brother)
Mervyn (Social worker)
Christine (Guardian)
Martha (Solicitor)
Police woman Jane
Policeman Jack

Peter's first picture

I started by drawing Peter in the middle, and his family around him, using an ordinary pencil. He suggested adding as 'important people' the police, social workers, myself, and the solicitor who had all played a part in the events which brought him into care.

Peter's mother and father were divorced, and his mother had remarried. Peter was currently staying with relatives, and the decision to be made was whether to recommend a Residence Order to his aunt and uncle, a Care Order to the local authority, or a Supervision Order and his return home. Peter was 11, and a very withdrawn child. He did respond to these drawings, having been previously very reluctant to express his preferences, and he later gave me permission to show them to the court.

Having listed the people he thought were important, I then asked him to draw lines between each person and himself describing how he felt about each one. Green felt tip was for someone *very* important to him, blue for someone *quite* important, and red for someone *not* important to him (I avoided using more emotionally loaded words such as love, like and hate). The results surprised me, as I had expected more attachment to his real father and less to his stepfather, but he confirmed that he had drawn what he really felt.

Peter's second picture

The next week I showed Peter his picture again, and he did not want to change it. I explained that I would like to know more about where he used to live, and what he thought about his future. I drew a winding path with him walking along it, from babyhood to manhood, and helped him mark off significant changes. I asked if he would still like to be with Auntie Sue and Uncle Peter at Christmas (yes), at Easter (yes), and next Christmas. It gradually emerged that he wanted to stay with his relatives permanently, but he had found it very hard to show what he felt was disloyalty to his mother.

Peter's relatives reported that he was initially upset after my visit, but then relieved that his feelings were out in the open. He did not change his mind when the solicitor subsequently talked to him about his pictures, and the court made an order allowing him to remain with his aunt and uncle.

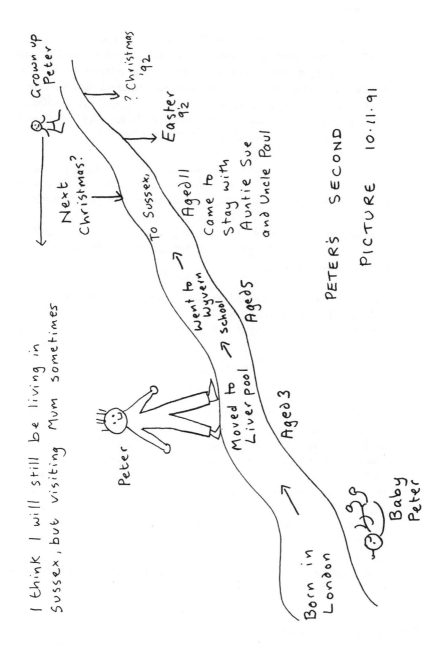

I think I will still be living in Sussex, but visiting Mum sometimes

Grown up Peter

Next Christmas?

? Christmas '92

Easter '92

To Sussex,

Aged 11
Came to
Stay with
Auntie Sue
and Uncle Paul

Went to
Wyvern
school

Aged 5

Peter

Moved to
Liverpool

Aged 3

Born in
London

Baby
Peter

PETER'S SECOND

PICTURE 10·11·91

Lucy's book

Lucy was a girl of 11 with learning difficulties. She was the eldest child of a large family and often had to look after her little brothers and sisters. Her father had left home in the previous year. The family lived in poverty, and their standards of child care were very poor. Lucy was thought to be in danger because she associated with certain men on her estate known to have offended against children, and her mother was unable to control her.

Lucy settled into her foster home very happily and appeared to revel in the freedom from responsibility and having clean clothes to wear. However, her father, his parents and her mother all wanted to have Lucy back. I wanted to assess Lucy's feelings about each of these people, but her learning difficulties made it hard for her to give consistent replies—she tended to say what she thought people expected of her.

I noticed that Lucy enjoyed having stories read to her, and asked if she would like to make a book about herself. She enjoyed making a pretty cover, but tended to lose interest when we were writing, until I started 'rewarding' her with coloured stickers saying 'well done' or 'very good'. She was allowed to choose one at the end of each session.

I then wrote down what Lucy told me about her family, and why she thought she was away from them (which revealed a very limited understanding). We then made a page for each family member and the foster parents, and listed the pros and cons of Lucy living with any of them in the future. By dividing the work into very short sessions like this, Lucy was able to concentrate, and could be reminded of what she had written previously. Her lists of 'pros and cons' was very revealing. She would miss her brothers and sisters if she stayed with the foster mother, but believed her father when he had promised 'a new house' if she went to him. Lucy and I showed the book to the solicitor when he visited, and used it as the basis of our recommendation to court.

Using outline drawings

There are a number of pre-drawn sketches available for therapeutic use with children, such as *The Anti-Colouring Book* (by Striker and

Kimmel, published by Hippo Books) or those published by BAAF such as *Talking Pictures* by Philip King. There are further examples at the end of this book on pages 108–112. These can be used with small children just to colour in while they are talking, or for older children to lead in to a discussion about their wishes and feelings. Some titles, such as 'my worst fears' or 'what upsets me most', may be over-intrusive or leading, with the inherent legal dangers of such an approach. However, subjects such as 'my three best wishes' or 'the people I would like to take on holiday with me' can provide a useful jumping-off point.

I have used this sort of outline drawing with older children who are used to being set written assignments for homework. They need to be quite competent and motivated to complete a task like this, but may prefer to think about what is being asked of them between interviews rather than working in front of the guardian or solicitor. A young person may also be encouraged to write a letter or make a tape recording to say how they feel, but whatever the finished article, it should be used with sensitivity, and the young person consulted before it is shown to anyone else.

Therapy with children

Some of the child clients of guardians and solicitors may also have received specialist help from a child psychiatrist or play therapist, who may have used more sophisticated techniques than those described above. Although guardians have a social work background and may feel drawn to therapeutic work with a vulnerable child client, this is outside the remit given by the court and can actually be unhelpful to the child, who may become attached to someone who cannot sustain the contact after the case is concluded. Children in these circumstances have often been let down by a number of adults, and it is necessary to be aware of the danger of inviting a dependence that cannot be maintained.

Psychotherapists are trained to interpret the art work or play activities of children in more depth than most guardians would feel capable of doing. Similarly, the use of so-called 'anatomically correct' dolls in work with children who have been sexually abused is best left to professionals who have been specially trained, as misleading interpretations can sometimes be made which would not withstand the scrutiny of cross-examination. Using ordinary toys and drawing materials are usually just as successful for solicitors and guardians, and clear observation and reporting of the child's responses should be readily understood by the court without a high degree of interpretation.

What the solicitor can use in direct work with children

Much of the direct work with the child will be undertaken by the guardian, who will then share her conclusions with the solicitor. It might be helpful for him to sit in on some of these sessions, either observing or taking a more active part. It is also a good idea for the guardian to show any written material produced by the child to the solicitor, with the child's agreement, which can form the basis of his instructions.

Some solicitors may want to adopt some of the suggestions outlined above to take a more pro-active approach with their child clients. This would be appropriate if they are taking separate instructions, or if there is a delay in the appointment of a guardian. It would in any case be a good idea to have a basic kit to use with children who are waiting in court. This could consist of drawing materials, simple games or a pack of cards, and some outline drawings including one of the court to explain the layout and personnel. Examples are set out on pages 108–112.

If visiting a child in a foster home or school, it may be easier to use books or toys at hand rather than taking one's own. Most young children enjoy being read to, and questions about the child's own feelings can then arise quite naturally from the text. I use a small paperback picture book called *Smith the Lonely Hedgehog* published and written by Althea to explore the subject of making friends and then having to move on, and another called *Ooh, I Feel Awful* by Whitney, published by Collins Picture Lions, about a boy waiting to see the school nurse and dreading the unknown. I prefer to use stories about animals, or everyday childhood experiences rather than 'socially aware' titles along the lines of *I am in Care* or *My Mother has a Drink Problem* which I feel might suggest ways of thinking which are not necessarily the child's own.

Photographs

Another invaluable aid to work with children are photographs if they are available. Both adults and children usually enjoy looking at photos of past events and describing who is in them. If a child has been in care for some time and is being prepared for adoption, it would be good practice for the social worker to have compiled a 'life story book' for the child. This would consist of photos of his natural parents and other family members if available, pictures and descriptions of other places the child has lived, and personal details such as when he cut his first tooth or who came to a birthday party. There may also be a simple account of events in the child's life and reasons why he is going to have a new mummy and daddy. These life story books fulfil an important function in giving a child without strong family ties some notion of a past on which to build future understanding and relationships. Even looking at photos of other children in a foster home can be a good way of opening up discussion with a child about himself or his family.

Whatever means the solicitor chooses to use in his work with child clients, it is important to feel comfortable and unselfconscious. It is a good idea to try several different approaches until something that is suitable for this particular child becomes apparent. It is also worth trying out unfamiliar methods and ideas to unlock the barriers to communication with a child client.

CHAPTER 4

Gathering information

After their initial meeting to discuss how to manage the case, the guardian and solicitor are likely to pursue different objectives for the next few weeks. The guardian will be gathering information about the case from Social Service records, interviews with the child, his family, foster parents, teachers, health visitors and other interested people. The solicitor will be liaising with the local authority and the solicitor for the parents to examine the grounds for the proceedings, what witnesses are to be produced and by which party, and possibly enlisting the services of an expert witness. Any witness statements or other relevant documents will need to be shared and discussed with the guardian. The guardian and solicitor will keep in touch by telephone and letter and are likely to meet at directions hearings which they are both expected to attend (rule 16) in order to assist the court with timetabling, and issues that may arise concerning contact or consent to medical examinations. They may also meet on joint visits to the child.

Towards the end of the investigative phase of the case, it is helpful to both the guardian and the solicitor to arrange a further meeting to evaluate the information so far collected and to decide on the recommendation to be made to the court on behalf of the child. The material to be discussed is likely to include documents, case conference minutes, reports of interviews, witness statements and the observations and ideas of the guardian and solicitor. From this material it should be possible to start building a framework for the final recommendation. This will be based on:

(1)   the background history of the child and his family;

(2)   the events leading to the present proceedings;

(3)   the views of each party;

(4)   the child's own wishes and feelings;

(5)   the local authority's plan.

The background history of the child and his family

Child care cases vary in the amount of information that is already known about the child and his family. In some cases a crisis develops rapidly in a family that has apparently been functioning satisfactorily and has not previously come to the attention of the authorities. In these cases the guardian will have a lot of basic information to find out which will help her understand the background to the present problem, but the social worker and possibly other agencies such as the police will also be investigating, and it is important to minimise the stress on the family of too many callers asking the same questions.

It is more common for children coming before the courts to have a history of previous involvement with the Social Services. Some guardians prefer to meet the people concerned before reading the file, in case their view is coloured by what they have read. Other guardians start their investigations by reading the Social Services file at the outset. This can minimise the risk of alienating the family by asking clumsy questions (perhaps about a child who has died), and may also alert the guardian to any special circumstances she should be aware of before visiting. For example, social workers may have experienced violence or threats from the family and should not visit unaccompanied; the guardian might then use the solicitor's office for an interview, or ask him to attend. (Guardians working from home do have difficulties arranging interviews, because they lack office accommodation and are often reluctant to give out their home telephone numbers. Solicitors can be of great assistance if they or their secretaries are willing to pass on messages from clients who cannot keep appointments or who wish to contact the guardian.)

Although the Social Services file is likely to contain a wealth of information about the family and the Department's dealings with them, the guardian needs to treat this information with caution if she is to preserve her independence. Sometimes factual information is inaccurate, such as a date of birth, which needs to be checked with the parents. More often some hearsay allegations or impression given about a particular incident hardens into fact, and the subsequent actions of the local authority are based on an erroneous piece of information recorded many years previously. Now that clients have access to their personal files, with some limitations, under the Access to Personal Files Act, and guardians have the right to examine records (section 42), social workers are more aware of outside scrutiny of their notes. While this provides a safeguard against factually incorrect information, there are also likely to be fewer of the social workers' own opinions recorded, and the guardian may need to seek these verbally.

An average social service file is likely to contain a great quantity of case records, minutes of meetings, administrative forms and correspondence. It is easy to lose sight of the child in question amid all the history described, and a useful exercise to understand how particular events affected the child at different stages of his development is to write out a chronology such as the one below.

Charlie's life history

0 months:	Born prematurely, separated from mother at birth, and nursed in the special care baby unit.
1 week:	Mother is discharged, but visits Charlie daily at first, then less frequently.
4 weeks:	Charlie is discharged to the care of his mother, who is suffering from post-natal depression.
6 weeks:	The health visitor is concerned about Charlie's failure to thrive, and instigates a multi-disciplinary case conference. A family aide starts visiting Charlie's mother to help her with child care.

12 weeks:	The family aide reports bruising to Charlie's face. He is admitted to hospital and a further case conference is held. His name is put on the at risk register. Charlie is discharged home after a week and a social worker starts to visit.
9 months:	Charlie's mother is managing better, and appears to have established a good bond with him. His height and weight gain are satisfactory.
15 months:	Mother has a new boyfriend and is pregnant again. She is irritable with Charlie and asks for help with him. The social worker contacts Charlie's grandmother who agrees to have him for a holiday.
18 months:	Charlie is still with his grandmother. His mother is having a difficult pregnancy and cannot have him back.
20 months:	Charlie's grandmother has a heart attack, and he is placed with a short-term foster mother, who lives a long way from Charlie's home town. The social worker encourages his mother to visit, but it is difficult for her in the final stages of pregnancy.
2 years:	The social worker tries to reintroduce Charlie to his family with a series of visits and overnight stays. Charlie is spiteful to the new baby, and only barely tolerated by his stepfather, who has a history of offences against children.
2yrs 6m:	The social worker concludes that rehabilitation has failed, and Charlie is made the subject of a Care Order.
2yrs 8m:	A case conference decides to place Charlie for adoption. He has now been with his foster mother for a year and has become very attached to her.
3 years:	Charlie is moved to prospective adopters. His behaviour is very disturbed. He has nightmares, soils himself frequently and is cruel to the family's pets. After a month the placement breaks down, and Charlie is moved to another short-term foster home.

3yrs 6m: Charlie's mother has split up from her boyfriend, and seems to be bringing up her second child successfully. She applies to the court for revocation of the Care Order and seeks to have Charlie returned to her.

Another method of highlighting disruption in a child's life is to compile a bar chart using different colours each time there is a significant change in the caring arrangements, which graphically shows the degree of continuity or lack of it.

From the chronology outlined above, it can clearly be seen how certain events that occurred at a critical stage in Charlie's development affected his subsequent behaviour. He was born prematurely, and separated from his mother for the first four weeks of his life. With hindsight it seems doubtful that she ever bonded to him at birth. From then he spent the next 14 months of his life with his mother, at a stage of his development when he would be naturally forming a strong attachment to his primary caregiver (in this case, his mother). This attachment was broken by his removal to his grandmother. He subsequently became attached again to his foster mother, and was then separated from her a year later, when he had spent half of his life in her care. His subsequent disturbance is not surprising, and indicates the emotional damage he has suffered by being uprooted yet again. The guardian and solicitor now have to assess the likelihood of further harm to Charlie if he returns to his mother, or what is likely to happen to him if he remains in care.

The events leading to the present proceedings

The guardian and solicitor will want to examine the events leading to the commencement of the current proceedings as these might be in dispute in a contested hearing. The guardian will compare the version written up in the Social Services file with the social worker's first witness statement, and with the account given by the parents or other people involved. She will want to know if the harm suffered by the child has been cumulative, or the result of a sudden crisis, and whether the actions of the local authority have been appropriate. A description of two contrasting cases illustrates the different approach that might be taken by the social workers concerned.

Kirsty and Kieran—did the Social Services over-react?

Case A: Gary and Lynn were a young unmarried couple with a baby girl, Kirsty, who was nine months old, and Kieran who was two. They were on the fringes of a hippy/drug sub-culture and reacted negatively to authority. The day nursery attended by Kieran reported that he was usually well cared for, bright for his age, and always pleased to see his parents when they fetched him.

The couple were not known to the Social Services until they split up, and Lynn went to a women's refuge alleging that Gary had been violent to her. She left the children with him because she did not want Kieran to lose his nursery place, and she thought they were better off in their own home than in the refuge. Some weeks later the nursery reported some injuries to Kieran which the doctor thought were non-accidental, and he was taken into care under the terms of a Place of Safety Order (CYPA 1969). Gary was drunk when the social worker visited him to inform him what had happened, and was abusive. Kirsty was taken away from him, although she appeared to be well. Thereafter the social worker did not visit again, but wrote letters inviting Gary to the office to discuss the case. He made no attempt to contact Lynn, assuming that she was an irresponsible mother for leaving the children as she did.

The guardian and solicitor were not appointed until a week later, after the court had made an Interim Care Order on both children for a further month. The guardian visited the children in a foster home in the next county (there was a local shortage, and Kirsty and Kieran had been placed some 30 miles away from their home). The guardian was disturbed to find both children in a very poor state. They seemed to have no appetite, were sleeping badly, and were clingy and tearful. Neither parent had visited, and the children seemed to be showing clear signs of separation trauma.

The guardian located the mother at the refuge, and she was unaware of what had happened. She had her own room, and the management of the hostel were willing for her to have the children, and provided the necessary bedding. The guardian was so concerned about the effect on the children of further separation from their mother that she asked the solicitor to request the court to bring forward the next hearing. He successfully opposed a further Interim Care Order on the grounds that the mother was willing and able to have her children with her.

41

Terry and Angie's children—were the Social Services too slow to act?

Case B: Terry and Angie were a couple with learning difficulties who had four children under the age of three (including twins). They had both spent many years in institutions, and had little idea of how to look after children. The Social Services had supported the family to a high degree, with daily nursery places for three of the children and a daily visit from a family support worker to get the children ready to go out in the mornings. Terry and Angie and the children also attended a Family Centre run by a voluntary child care agency once a week where they were given help and advice with their budget and parenting skills.

Despite this high degree of assistance the children failed to thrive. The baby was not gaining weight properly, and the family support worker frequently found no food in the cupboard, and wet bedding—the children had chronic nappy rash and chest infections. The social worker was fond of Terry and Angie and felt they were like children themselves. Although she acknowledged that no amount of propping-up would improve conditions for the children, she felt it would be too cruel to their parents to remove them. The guardian and children's solicitor considered that the children were suffering too much harm by remaining with their parents, and recommended a Care Order.

These two contrasting cases point up the dilemmas for social workers, who in the face of public criticism feel they can never succeed. Guardians who have been social workers themselves can sympathise, but must try and be objective about the service offered to a family by the local authority. In Case A they fulfilled their duty to protect the children, but did not properly examine all the alternatives, which could have enabled them to be reunited with their mother at an earlier stage. The children suffered emotional damage as a result. In Case B, the social worker had become so committed to sustaining the family as a unit, that she failed to see the chronic physical and emotional harm endured by the children of such inadequate parents. The guardian and solicitor must always be guided by the principle that the welfare of *this* child is paramount, whatever the practice or policy of the local authority in general towards the children and families they serve.

The views of each party

As well as seeing the child, the guardian is likely to spend some time listening to the views of the parents, other family members, foster parents and other professionals and weighing up what each has to say about the child, and what should happen to him or her.

The child's parents

The parents may start off feeling hostile towards the guardian, seeing her as yet another authority figure lumped in with the Social Services and courts as being responsible for their child being taken away. Sometimes however, if parents can accept that the guardian is only concerned with what is best for their child, they may be able to positively assist her in her investigations. The parents are usually the best people to fill in the details of the child's background—whether his birth was normal, what he was like as a baby, any health problems and notable events that have affected him since then. The guardian can also learn a lot about the parents' current attitude to their child in the way they recount these things. Their view of what should happen in the future is likely to be strongly influenced by their own needs, and family pressures. It is not acceptable in our society to readily give up one's children or to acknowledge the inability to be a good-enough parent. Some may tacitly allow the proceedings to continue without putting up much opposition, preferring to leave other people to make a decision that is too painful to make for themselves.

Mrs. Morgan—an impossible choice

Mrs. Morgan had had a difficult childhood, and eventually married a man much older than herself to escape from home. He had psychiatric problems, and the marriage was a disaster, but Mrs. Morgan felt trapped within it. When Mr. Morgan died unexpectedly, Mrs. Morgan felt a great sense of release, and started an active social life. She met a man who wanted her to live with him, but did not want her children. Mrs. Morgan could not bring herself to choose between her boyfriend and children, but a series of 'misunderstandings' on her part led to them coming into care through being left on their own in the house. At first it looked as if this had happened because Mrs. Morgan was still under stress following her bereavement, but she doggedly refused to see the guardian, social worker or her own solicitor over a period of several months, and eventually the court accepted that she had indeed 'given up' her children to all intents and purposes, and had no alternative but to make a Care Order.

As well as the parents, other family members can often have a lot of insight into what has happened. Older brothers and sisters may have experienced similar treatment and have strong views about what should happen. In families where the parents are separated, the guardian may need to seek out an absent father and discuss with the child's solicitor whether he should be made a party to the proceedings, or if any other person has parental responsibility for the child within the meaning of the Children Act (section 2).

Grandparents

Grandparents often play a significant and under-rated part in the lives of their grandchildren. Social workers often do not get round to seeing them if they are not currently involved with the family, and the grandparents may be reluctant to interfere or get in touch themselves. Guardians tend to have more time to investigate and often find that grandparents have a great deal to offer. They can shed light on the history of the family and the relationships within it, and may be able to offer practical assistance with the child, either complementing a foster home, or by taking on full responsibility, though this may need to be supported financially or with other services such as day nursery provision. Social workers are sometimes reluctant to place children with relatives, fearing that this will cause bad feeling within the family, or that the grandparents must have been inadequate in some way themselves to have produced children who are not good parents to the child in question. This denies the possibility of change and maturation, let alone the often random nature of whether children grow up to be effective parents whatever their upbringing. Research has shown that children placed with relatives tend to do better than those in foster care, so this possibility should certainly be canvassed. Grandparents may also need legal advice because in certain circumstances they too can be made parties to the proceedings.

Foster carers

Other people consulted by the guardian might include foster carers, teachers and health visitors. Foster carers are well placed to comment on the day to day behaviour of the child and are more likely than anyone else to know what he feels about his own home. Foster carers have to cope with the child's distress or testing behaviour, and have to pick up the pieces if a visit from a guardian or solicitor further upsets him. It is important to acknowledge the crucial role of the foster carers, and to keep them informed of the progress of the case, so that they can fully support the child. There may be cases where it is appropriate for foster carers to be joined as parties, where for example they hope to adopt the child, or more unusually if they are opposed to the local authority plans for the child and have an alternative proposal.

Teachers

With children of school age, teachers are an invaluable source of information. They can describe the child's development and whether he is achieving his potential, and what his behaviour is like towards adults and other children. The child may also have revealed his feelings about his situation to his teacher, either overtly or through written or art work.

Maggie—a revealing episode at school

Maggie, aged five, had been in care for a year after sustaining serious injuries at the hands of her mother's boyfriend. The circumstances of these events were unclear, and it was not known how much her mother knew what was happening at the time.

Maggie suffered nightmares, but was unable to tell her foster mother what was troubling her. The guardian had been appointed because her mother had applied for contact. The guardian was unsure how much Maggie remembered about the past, and whether her mother was still significant to her. However, the teacher described an incident in school where she had asked the class to do a project on 'memories'. Maggie had become extremely agitated, saying she did not want to remember 'bad things'. This description helped the guardian to understand that Maggie did indeed remember the traumatic events that led to her reception into care, but that she had largely suppressed them and now required therapeutic assistance in coming to terms with what had happened to her if she were to fully recover.

Health visitors

Health visitors are key professionals in assessing the development of children under five. They have universal access to families with young children, but no statutory right of entry, so are understandably reluctant to lose the good will of the parents they visit. In some areas, health visitors will not speak to guardians unless accompanied by their nursing officers, and almost always need to be subpoenaed to give evidence.

Health visitors weigh and measure babies and young children at regular intervals, and record these measurements on centile charts. (A centile chart is reproduced in *Babyhood* by Penelope Leach.) These charts show the normal growth curves for the population as a whole (which are different for boys and girls) so the child can be compared with others of a similar age. As well as weight gain, measurements are taken of height (not very reliably in a curled-up baby) and head circumference. After accounting for parental size and short-term illness, the health visitor can assess whether the child is growing properly. The average growth curve is on the 50th centile; a big child might be on the 97th centile, and a small one on the 3rd centile, which would mean that only three per cent of the whole child population of his age would be smaller than him. This is acceptable if he comes from a family of short, slight people, or if he was premature for example, but would be worrying if it was an indication of poor nourishment. Another danger sign is if the child's growth curve starts flattening or even turning downwards, which indicates that he is not gaining weight and might even be losing it. As well as suggesting inadequate feeding, some children fail to grow properly because of emotional deprivation.

Tina—a child who failed to thrive

Tina, aged four, was the middle of three children. Her older brother was favoured by her mother, and a handicapped younger sister needed a great deal of care. Tina was close to her father but seemed to be rejected by her mother. The parents had a volatile marriage, with frequent separations and reconciliations. It became apparent that Tina's father feared for her safety if he was out of the home, and that Tina's mother both resented her husband's affection for the child, but was also prepared to use Tina to get him back. There were numerous reports of small cruelties perpetrated against the child, but the most significant sign of her distress was her failure to thrive. The nursery reported that Tina ate ravenously, and had been observed taking left-over food from the dustbins, but the social worker had seen Tina's mother serving up wholesome meals when she had called at the home unannounced. The health visitor was weighing Tina once a fortnight at the day nursery, and recorded a progressive decline in her growth curve.

The guardian and Tina's solicitor were sure that she was being rejected by her mother and suffering severe emotional deprivation, but it was a difficult case to prove. The solicitor asked a paediatrician who specialised in growth deficiencies to act as an expert witness. He examined Tina and concluded that her emotional suffering was preventing her absorption of nutrition, a rare phenomenon but one that seemed to be occurring in this case. The court accepted this evidence, and Tina was eventually adopted.

As well as measuring children's growth, health visitors also carry out developmental checks at regular intervals, to test the child's manual dexterity, co-ordination, sight and hearing. This screening service provides an early warning system to identify children with learning difficulties or health defects requiring treatment. The health visitor can indicate whether the child is developing normally, and whether his parents are up to date with immunisations and are able to seek medical help when appropriate. This might be a useful pointer where it is proposed that the child should remain at home as long as the parents can respond to social work help and supervision.

A general knowledge of normal childhood development would be helpful to solicitors practising in this field. There are many excellent baby and child care manuals generally available. A classic description of children's normal developmental milestones can be found in the 'Sheridan's Charts' reproduced in *Protecting Children*, HMSO, 1988—see the recommended reading list on page 103.

The child's own wishes and feelings

As well as gathering information about the family and the views of people who know them, the guardian and solicitor will pay particular attention to the views of the child himself, and this aspect should be covered by a separate heading in the guardian's report to the court. The weight to be given to the child's expressed wishes will increase the older he or she is, but even babies and young children can show their contentment or otherwise by their behaviour (such as Kieran and Kirsty in Case A described on page 41). The guardian should be able to provide the court with a physical description of the child, or even a photograph if he is not to attend in person, an outline of significant events in his life (perhaps in the form of a chronology), observations of his present behaviour and a report of what the guardian thinks are the child's own wishes. It is helpful to the court to know on what basis the guardian has reached this conclusion, and she should be prepared to produce the child's drawings or describe play sessions that have informed her views. Sometimes she will have been unable to determine what the child himself wants, if he is too young or inarticulate, and then she might have to rely on circumstantial evidence, for example that he has apparently thrived in care, or conversely seems miserable away from his home. As well as reporting the child's wishes, the guardian should attempt to say what the child needs, based on generally recognised criteria as well as what is specific to him. There have been many attempts to describe the basic rights of all children, and to separate what is essential from what is merely desirable. However, most commentators would say the child must be fed, washed and clothed properly, must be protected from danger, must be loved, educated and allowed sufficient and appropriate independence to develop his own personality. In addition, the child client under consideration might have his own specific needs, for example to receive counselling about past events (such as Maggie, page 45), or to be placed in a racially similar foster home (if he is a black child).

Taking separate instructions

The solicitor will be especially alert to the possibility of taking separate instructions from the child. Rule 12 is not specific about when this is appropriate, but states that it is when 'the solicitor considers, having taken into account the views of the guardian ad litem and any direction of the court . . ., that the child wishes to give instructions which conflict with those of the guardian ad litem and that he is able, having regard to his understanding, to give such instructions on his own behalf.' A benchmark case was that of Gillick v. West Norfolk and Wisbech Area Health Authority and the DHSS [1986] A.C. 112, when the Law Lords ruled that a girl of 15 could give valid consent to medical treatment— in this case contraceptive advice, despite parental disapproval. This case, which has given rise to the expression, the 'Gillick competent' child, suggests that 15 would be an appropriate age for a young person to give separate instructions, if he was of normal intelligence, but it would be more difficult in the case of a child aged 10 or 11. Two contrasting cases illustrate the difficulties facing a solicitor making this decision.

Sally—how much should a 14-year-old be given responsibility for a risky decision?

Sally was a girl of 14 living with her mother and stepfather. The school reported several instances when she had unexplained bruising to her face, and she was eventually taken into care when she suffered a broken arm caused by her stepfather.

When the guardian met Sally's mother and stepfather, they described her as wilful and defiant. The stepfather admitted he had broken her arm, but said this occurred during a struggle when he was trying to prevent her going out late at night. Sally's mother supported her husband in trying to control the girl, and said she would have to mend her ways if she was to return home. The guardian believed there were too many tensions within the family for Sally to be safe from her stepfather's temper, but Sally herself was homesick and wanted to go home. In this instance, the solicitor decided that Sally was old enough to understand the risks involved, and accepted her instructions to oppose the guardian's recommendation of a Care Order.

Danny—immediate wishes or long-term welfare?

Danny was a boy of 11 from a large family which largely ignored him and let him do what he liked outside the home. He was discovered spending much of his time with a homosexual waiter who had his own accommodation at a nearby hotel. The guardian considered that Danny's parents were incapable of protecting their son and the boy himself wanted to stay at home and continue the relationship. The solicitor had to decide whether to accept Danny's instructions to oppose the guardian's recommendation of a Care Order. He discussed with the guardian what her views were concerning Danny's maturity and understanding, and concluded that although Danny could express his wishes clearly, he could not understand the long-term implications of what he wanted to do. The solicitor decided to support the guardian's recommendation, and not to take separate instructions from Danny.

The local authority's plan

As well as understanding the events that brought the child before the court in the first place, the guardian and solicitor need to make a critical evaluation of the local authority's plan for the future care of the child. The application forms lodged at the court when the proceedings were commenced should have included the local authority's proposals. These may be rather vague, such as 'We shall attempt rehabilitation', or 'An assessment will be undertaken to see if the child can go home'. The guardian needs to assess how realistic these objectives are, in what time scale they are to be achieved, and what resources the local authority can offer to make the plan work. For instance an attempt at rehabilitation may be built on a programme of visits between the child and his parents. They will need financial help with bus fares to visit him in the foster home, and practical assistance to clean up the house before the child can stay overnight. The parents, child and social worker should all know what they are trying to achieve, and this may be in the form of a written agreement that can be shown to the court. The guardian should be aware of the 'no delay' principle governing children's cases, and will seek a timetable for the local authority's programme. She will want to avoid the possibility of 'drift', or 'waiting to see what happens' if that means postponing decisions about the child. Research has shown that unless children are rehabilitated with their parents within the first six weeks of coming into care, their chances of returning home diminish very rapidly, and the intensity and quality of social work done in these early weeks has a considerable bearing on the eventual outcome. A high degree of contact between the child and his family is needed if the relationship is to be preserved, and the child restored home quickly. The Act makes a presumption of 'reasonable contact' between the child and his parents (section 34), and the guardian will examine the arrangements for this to take place and whether the frequency and nature of the meetings are in the child's interests. She may wish to seek the court's directions for contact to be varied in some way while the final outcome of the case is awaited.

The guardian will also want to know if the local authority has the resources to support any particular plan. If a child is to return home, it is important to know if a day nursery place can be made available or regular family support if this is required. The guardian may not feel able to recommend rehabilitation if there is a waiting list for such services. If a child is to remain in care, the guardian will want to examine the long-term plans for him. Is he to be placed for adoption, and if so how likely is it that a suitable family can be found? If he is to remain in foster care, what are the chances of him staying with the same people, or is he likely to be moved around? What plans are there for contact with his family to be maintained?

Case conferences

Apart from reading the files and discussing the case with the social worker and his or her manager, another means of discovering this sort of information is to attend any case conferences or planning meetings convened by the local authority. Guardians are often invited, solicitors less frequently, and guidance is offered in 'Working Together' on the appropriate circumstances for either to attend. The child's solicitor can be said to represent the child's interests, but other people attending may feel constrained if they think their comments could be quoted in court. The primary reason for a case conference is to enable the local authority to make a decision about its recommendation and the child's guardian and solicitor should not try to influence that decision, although they may have fresh information to share. Guardians are usually invited to attend as observers, and it is very useful to hear what the participants have to say, and to be able to see the process that leads to a particular outcome. It may be a unanimous decision, or there may be real dissent on the part of one or more people attending which may need exploration outside the conference. Solicitors should appreciate that individual social workers do not make casework decisions in isolation. Their managers are likely to influence policy on particular cases in the light of departmental guidelines, and the powerful inter-agency body that monitors the child protection procedures can veto decisions made at a more junior level. Guardians should have access to published social service departmental policy, and be able to advise the child's solicitor who are the key personnel who make decisions in a particular case, and who may be needed subsequently in court.

Having gathered as much information as possible, the guardian and solicitor now have to reach a joint decision what to recommend on behalf of the child and the solicitor whether, if he is mature enough, the child is capable of giving separate instructions. The guardian needs to prepare her report to be submitted to the court at least seven days before the hearing, and the solicitor needs to make his final preparations for the presentation of the case, which is dealt with in the following chapter.

CHAPTER 5

The final hearing

When the solicitor and guardian have discussed all the information available they need to reach a decision on what order or combination of orders to recommend, or whether it is in the child's best interests for no order to be made. There is a presumption in the Children Act that courts should only intervene when it can be demonstrated that making an order is better for the child than making no order at all, so that even if the grounds are proved, the local authority still has to justify the need for an order (section 1(5)). The underlying philosophy of the Act is for the concept of parental responsibility to be fostered and sustained, and that the state should only intervene when there is no alternative means of protecting the child and safeguarding his welfare.

If it can be shown that an order is needed, there is now the possibility of selecting the most appropriate order or combination of orders from a 'flexible menu', which allows the solicitor and guardian to design a custom-built recommendation for the needs of their child client rather than trying to squeeze his requirements into an inflexible and narrow choice of alternatives, as existed previously.

Summary of the orders available

(Solicitors will of course require more comprehensive knowledge of the Children Act than is provided here, but there is much interpretative material that is excellent—see the recommended reading list on page 103.)

In the early stages of the proceedings the protection of the child and an assessment of his needs can be secured by any of the following.

(1) Emergency Protection Order (section 44)

Can be made when the local authority has 'reasonable cause' to *believe* that the child is likely to suffer 'significant harm' unless he is removed from home, or secured in a safe place (e.g. hospital). The order lasts for up to eight days and can be renewed once. The parents or the child himself have the right of appeal after 72 hours unless they were present at the original hearing, and there is a presumption of reasonable contact unless the court directs otherwise.

(2) Child Assessment Order (section 43)

Can be made when the local authority has 'reasonable cause' to *suspect* that the child is suffering, or likely to suffer 'significant harm', that an assessment is needed to determine this issue, and that an order is needed to secure such an assessment. The order specifies the date on which the assessment is to begin, and lasts seven days from that date. The court can make directions relating to the assessment, and has to make directions as to contact if the child is to be kept away from home.

Note on consent

Solicitors should note that in either of these orders the child may 'if he is of sufficient understanding to make an informed decision' refuse to submit to a medical or psychiatric examination or other assessment (section 43(8) and section 44(7)). This provision is likely to cause some ethical dilemmas for the solicitor and guardian, who may believe that it is in the child's best interests to be examined, but who have the duty nevertheless to ensure that a mature child is giving his informed consent. It is questionable how much a child can be expected to understand in relation to the implications of a medical, for instance. A sympathetic doctor, guardian or solicitor can explain the procedures to a child where sexual abuse is suspected, but if the doctor is also collecting samples for forensic purposes, should it be explained that the outcome might result in the prosecution of the child's father, or the breakdown of the parents' marriage? These consequences might occur in any case, but the question still arises as to what is reasonable for a child to bear in the way of responsibility. It might be helpful to provide an analogy with a common childhood experience, that of visiting the dentist. A good parent would prepare the child by explaining what the dentist would do, and the consequences for the child's health if rotten teeth were not treated. Although the child might not relish the prospect, he or she would usually agree to attend, but in the final analysis could not be dragged to the dentist's chair against his will.

In the case of children giving consent to medicals or other examinations under the Act, they need to know what procedures will be used, and given a general explanation of the purpose of the examination. In a case where sexual abuse is suspected, there would be sound medical reasons, such as the detection of pregnancy or venereal disease, for which the child would need treatment or advice. The child in this instance could be told that the doctor was checking to make sure there was nothing wrong. The child's welfare would justify such an examination, and the person advising the child would not be promoting his or her welfare by drawing attention to the possible consequences for a third party. No child should be forced either emotionally or physically to submit to an examination, which in any case a doctor may rightly regard as tantamount to an assault. The whole area of children's consent is a sensitive and difficult issue, which may be helped by case law as the provisions of the Children Act are tested in practice.

On or before the expiry of either an Emergency Protection or Child Assessment Order, the court can, on application by the local authority under section 31, go on to make one or more of the following.

(3) Interim Care Order (section 38)

Can be made when there are reasonable grounds for believing that:

(a) the child is suffering, or likely to suffer, significant harm, and

(b) (i) that the harm is attributable to the care given to him 'not being what it would be reasonable to expect a parent to give to him' or

(ii) that he is beyond parental control.

These are known as the 'threshold criteria'. The order can last for up to eight weeks, and can be renewed at up to four-weekly intervals thereafter. Courts can only renew an Interim Order if satisfied that to do so is in the child's best interests and the threshold criteria still exist. As with all the other orders available, there is a presumption of reasonable contact unless the court directs otherwise. An Interim Care Order would allow the local authority to look after the child away from home. If they were satisfied that he would be safe at home during the period of an assessment they would probably seek an:

(4) Interim Supervision Order (section 38)

The grounds for this order are the same as those for an Interim Care Order but the responsibility for the child remains with the parents and he would normally stay at home or with another named person under a Residence Order. The supervisor (probably the local authority social worker) has the duty to 'advise, assist and befriend' the supervised child, and can take 'such steps as are reasonably necessary to give effect to the order'. This might be a requirement for the parents to attend appointments with the supervisor or, for instance, a health visitor, or to allow the child to join some activity provided by the Social Services such as a counselling group or an 'outward bound' type of organised holiday. The order lasts for up to eight weeks and can be renewed at up to four-weekly intervals. An Interim Supervision Order can be combined with one or more of the following.

(5) Section 8 orders

Residence Order

Individuals, such as grandparents, foster parents, or the child himself (with certain provisos) can apply for a Residence Order, determining with whom the child should live. Such an application could arise from private law proceedings, but a local authority is not allowed to apply for a Residence Order. The court can make a Residence Order of its own volition, even if the original application was for a different order, and this might be the recommendation of the guardian or solicitor. For example, the local authority might wish to place a child with an aunt, but would have to seek a Care Order as it is not itself permitted to apply for a Residence Order. The aunt may be willing to accept responsibility for the child, but unwilling for reasons of the expense and trouble involved, to apply for a Residence Order herself. In this case, the guardian could recommend the court to make a Residence Order to the aunt. A Residence Order may be made for a specified period, and this provision could be useful in cases where the guardian and solicitor wished to test a particular course of action before making a final recommendation.

Contact Order

A section 8 Contact Order may be sought concerning a child not in the care of the local authority. (Contact with these children is governed by section 34 and discussed on page 57.) Although a local authority may not apply for a section 8 Contact Order another party could apply within the public law proceedings or the court of its own motion may make a section 8 Contact Order.

Section 8 Contact Orders are also likely to be used in private law proceedings by parents, step parents or grandparents wanting contact with a child no longer living with them. A section 8 Contact Order may also be sought (with the leave of the court) by a child of 'sufficient understanding', who might, for example, want contact with his father but is being prevented by his mother with whom he is living.

Prohibited Steps Order

This may be sought to prevent a particular course of action such as the removal of a child from the country. The local authority is entitled to apply and there have been instances where this provision has been used to exclude a suspected abuser from a household, rather than removing the children. There are, however, problems of enforcement, and at such an early stage in the implementation of the Children Act the use of this order in such cases is still controversial and uncertain.

Specific Issue Order

This can be used to remedy a particular problem, and can be applied for by the local authority. This order could be sought to allow a child to have medical treatment such as a life-saving blood transfusion where the parents might refuse on religious grounds.

(It should be noted that applications for section 8 orders, where there are no public law (e.g. care) proceedings afoot, do not come within the 'specified proceedings' for which a guardian and solicitor for the child are normally appointed. The Court Welfare Service may be asked by the court to prepare a report in these circumstances; or in exceptional cases the local authority could be asked to investigate. In the latter case, a guardian and solicitor for the child can be appointed.)

(6) Care Order (section 33)

A full Care Order may be made if the same 'threshold criteria' outlined above for an Interim Care Order are met, and the court is satisfied that it would be better for the child to make such an order rather than an alternative or no order at all. A Care Order lasts until the child is 18 (unless the court discharges it earlier), and creates joint parental responsibility between the parents and the local authority, though section 33(3) allows the local authority to determine the extent to which parents meet their parental responsibility.

Contact with children subject to Care Orders

Section 34(1) makes the presumption that the local authority will allow the child reasonable contact with his parents. Subsection (3) allows an application for contact with or from any other named person with the leave of the court. There are additional provisions to enable the court to make directions with respect to contact, or to terminate it altogether. Section 34(9) allows for variation or discharge of any order concerning contact, and section 34(10) permits the court to make an order either at the same time as the Care Order or later. Section 34(11) states that the court 'shall consider' the arrangements made for contact before making a Care Order, and it is clearly the intention of the Act that there should be a plan for continuing contact between parents and child, or sound reasons concerning the well-being of the child if it is to be curtailed or terminated. The guardian and solicitor should give the court their recommendations concerning the frequency and nature of the contact between the child and each person who is significant to him (e.g. parents, other relations or previous carers), and any other observations about contact, such as the most suitable venue, and whether or not it should be supervised. Contact does not necessarily imply face-to-face meetings, but may include letters, telephone calls or sending photographs and information about the child's progress.

(7) Supervision Order (section 35)

A Supervision Order can be made where the 'threshold criteria' are met. The child's parents retain parental responsibility. The supervisor shall 'advise, assist and befriend' the child, and can ask for conditions to be attached to the order, such as a requirement for the child to be weighed by a health visitor at stated intervals. A Supervision Order lasts for one year, but may be renewed by the court for up to a further two years.

(8) Education Supervision Order (section 36)

Made on the application of a local education authority, to assist a child whose school attendance is unsatisfactory.

(9) Family Assistance Order (section 16)

This can only be made on the court's own motion, but can be made in any family proceedings. It lasts for six months, and is only to be made in exceptional circumstances. It requires the local authority or probation service to make an officer available to 'advise, assist and befriend' the person named in the order who may be the child himself, his parent, the person he lives with, or someone who has a contact order in respect of the child. The person named must agree to the making of the order, unless he is the child, as must the local authority. This short-term order may be used to help a newly divorced parent through a difficult transitional period, and to some extent is intended to replace the old Matrimonial Supervision Orders. It recognises that an adult rather than the child may be the focus of assistance in a troubled family, and would be more appropriate than making the child himself subject to a Supervision Order.

Children 'in need'

Solicitors should also be aware of the provisions of Part III of the Act which impose wide-ranging duties on the local authority to provide services for children 'in need'. This includes, for example, day care or the provision of 'accommodation' for children whose parents cannot care for them for whatever reason, but who are agreeable to the local authority 'looking after' the child on their behalf. This latter provision takes over from the old 'voluntary care' arrangements. Provision of Part III services may mean that there is no need for a Care Order.

It can be seen from the range of orders available that the solicitor and guardian may 'mix and match' to obtain the most appropriate combination of orders to meet the needs of their child client. If we return to the hypothetical case of Charlie, whose chronology was outlined in Chapter 4, page 38, the recommendation might be for the court to make a time-limited section 34 Contact Order directing the local authority to set up regular meetings between Charlie and his mother, while the possibility of re-establishing their relationship can be examined. At the end of a three-month period, the child's solicitor may support the mother's request for a six-month Residence Order, but recommend that a Supervision Order is made to run concurrently, with a direction that Charlie's mother should allow the social worker to see Charlie once a week, and to take him to the day nursery twice a week.

After six months the court may be satisfied that Charlie no longer requires supervision, and that the Residence Order can lapse in favour of his mother regaining full parental responsibility. If the process went wrong at any stage, the local authority could intervene with an application for an Interim Care Order or (if extremely urgent) an Emergency Protection Order; or an offer of accommodation if the mother was agreeable. This step-by-step approach is more likely to be effective in restoring Charlie to his mother on a planned basis, rather than the abrupt discharge of the Care Order without the possibility of a carefully planned and supervised return.

Factors influencing the guardian in her recommendations

Having collected as much information about the case as is available, and after discussion with the solicitor about the weight of the evidence and the range of possible orders, the guardian has to decide what she thinks is in the child's best interests. Her thinking is likely to be influenced by her experience of similar child care cases, by research findings and by several concepts familiar to social workers that have evolved over the years, and can be contradictory. There is, for instance, a body of knowledge concerned with the protection of the child from dangerous parents, but also a recognition that the risk of foster care breakdown is high (33–50 per cent) and that institutional care can also be very detrimental, with a rapid turnover of staff, many of whom are young or inadequately trained and supported. There have also been a number of recent cases revealing institutionalised abuse of children in care. Similarly much child care literature emphasises the importance of permanence in children's lives and the need to plan long-term alternative care if there is insufficient attachment between children and their natural parents. There is also recognition that children need family ties to develop a sense of identity and self-esteem. The guardian should consider in the case of more than one child whether their need to be together outweighs the benefits each may derive from separate placement (see the example of Ryan and Tracey in Chapter 1, page 8), remembering that *each child* is a separate client, and they are not necessarily best served by being treated alike. The guardian may recognise the child's attachment to his family, and the emotional harm he would suffer if parted from them, but she might also consider he would be at risk of injury if he remained with them. Where there has been gross cruelty or rejection it may be easier to reach a conclusion than in the majority of cases, where there is a fine balance between the advantages to the child of maintaining him in the family, as against the dangers of failure to remove him from home.

Children Act definitions

The guardian also has to wrestle with the concept of 'good-enough' parenting. This phrase does not appear in the Act, but reflects the idea that most parents meet most of their children's needs most of the time, but others fall short of this. It is recognised that parents who are poor, ill-educated or physically handicapped may not be able to do such a good job of bringing up their children as more privileged families, but the problem is to define what is acceptable or not for the child. The Act talks about 'significant harm' suffered by the child when compared to the health and development of a 'similar child' (section 31(10)). This may allow for the effect of handicap, parental disability or class and racial differences in bringing up children, but the Guidance states that 'the standard appropriate for the child in question' must be used (para. 3.20 of Volume One). The Act also says that the harm must be attributable to the care not being what it would be 'reasonable to expect a parent' to give (or that the child is beyond parental control). There may well need to be some test cases before the 'reasonable parent' and 'significant harm' can be properly defined.

Pragmatic considerations

As well as considering these various factors, the guardian also has to weigh up the ideal solution for the child against what is reasonably achievable. There is a sense in which guardians should critically appraise the performance of the local authority in order to improve their service to this particular child in the future. Sometimes the observations of the guardian or solicitor in court can bring pressure to bear on the local authority who will then comply with their recommendations, but it has to be remembered that the guardian and solicitor are only involved for a limited period before the management of the case reverts completely to the Social Services. The guardian has to make a realistic assessment of what can be achieved for the child given the resources and personnel that are actually available. To return to the example of Charlie, a successful reunification of the family would depend on the availability of staff to arrange visits, to escort or pay fares for the mother, and to supervise the contact. There would also need to be a nursery place available within reasonable distance of Charlie's home. If the social worker found it difficult to support the plan, or there was a changeover of staff, or a freeze on the Social Services budget, the guardian may decide that an attempt to return Charlie had a low chance of success, and that his security could be better achieved by another attempt at adoption.

The 'welfare checklist'

The Children Act, s. 1(3) instructs the court to 'have regard' to a list of factors known as the 'welfare checklist' when considering whether to make, vary or discharge a section 8, Care or Supervision Order. These are:

(a) the ascertainable wishes and feelings of the child concerned (considered in the light of his age and understanding);

(b) his physical, emotional and educational needs;

(c) the likely effect on him of any change in his circumstances;

(d) his age, sex, background and any characteristics of his which the court considers relevant;

(e) any harm which he has suffered or is at risk of suffering;

(f) how capable each of his parents and any other person in relation to whom the court considers the question to be relevant, is of meeting his needs;

(g) the range of powers available to the court under this Act in the proceedings in question.

Issues of religion, race, language and culture

All these matters should be covered by the guardian, either under separate headings (which may make it more cumbersome to read), or in the main body of her report. It should be noted that paragraph (d) of the checklist allows for consideration of the child's racial needs; there is a specific duty on the local authority in other parts of the Act (e.g. section 22(5)(c)) to 'give due consideration to the child's religious persuasion, racial origin and cultural and linguistic background'. When the child client is from an ethnic minority or is of mixed parentage the guardian should draw the attention of the court to his need to maintain links with his own culture, e.g. by placement with foster parents of similar racial origins, or the need to safeguard his religious observances by placement with practising members of the same faith. In working with families whose first language is not English, the guardian and solicitor may need to employ an interpreter but this can be difficult. In a small community the interpreter might already know the family, and the issue of confidentiality then arises. There is also the need to balance the child's racial needs with other considerations, e.g. whether keeping sibling groups of black children together is only possible if they are placed in a white family. The delay resulting from a search for a suitable same-race family might not be justifiable, if the child is becoming attached to his existing carers of a different race.

Secure accommodation

For the first time, under section 25 of the Act, a guardian can now be appointed on behalf of a young person when the local authority has applied to the Family Proceedings Court for a Secure Accommodation Order in non-criminal cases, or in remand cases in the Crown Court. (The majority of young people held in secure accommodation are either remanded for criminal offences or placed under section 53 of the Children and Young Persons Act 1933 and guardians are not appointed to these cases.) The solicitor instructed by the guardian on behalf of the child might well be more familiar with this type of proceeding. The grounds for a secure accommodation order are that the child:

(a) (i) has a history of absconding and is likely to abscond from any other description of accommodation; and

(ii) if he absconds, he is likely to suffer significant harm; or

(b) that if he is kept in any other description of accommodation he is likely to injure himself or other persons.

As in other proceedings under the Children Act, the child's welfare must be the paramount consideration, but there is also the need to consider the safety of others. As well as examining the history of absconding, dangerous behaviour or self harm committed by the young person which might justify an order, the guardian should also be able to support the local authority's submission that no alternative provision would safely contain the child if she is to recommend a Secure Accommodation Order.

This type of proceeding might well involve the solicitor taking separate instructions from the young person who is likely to be of sufficient 'understanding' to give them. It would be exceptional for a child under the age of 13 to be held in secure accommodation as the Secretary of State must agree to such a placement for this age group. The young person is unlikely to want to be locked up even if the guardian considers there is no alternative way of keeping him or others safe.

Solicitors should be aware of the very strict rules governing the operation of secure accommodation, and be prepared to advise their young client of his rights to have the placement reviewed and to have an independent visitor if he is not in touch with his family. Young people in secure accommodation may be isolated from sources of help and advice because of distance, and would benefit from being told how to contact the solicitor in case of future need.

The solicitor's preparation for the final hearing

In preparing his case on behalf of the child for the final hearing the solicitor needs to consider the following:

(a) the evidence;

(b) the law;

(c) witnesses;

(d) disclosure of the reports;

(e) preparation of the child.

(a) The evidence

To prove its case and to establish the 'threshold criteria' for the making of an order, the local authority will produce a statement from one or more social workers concerning the events that triggered the present proceedings. There may be additional evidence from day nursery staff or family aide workers, teachers, health visitors or doctors. For example, day nursery staff, after consultation with a social worker, may call a community medical officer (CMO) to examine a child if they suspect that bruises, scratches, burns or other marks may have been caused non-accidentally. A CMO would record his or her findings in detail, along with drawings of the site and extent of the injuries. She might refer the child for a second opinion or more extensive screening to the paediatric department of the local hospital. Initial diagnosis of non-accidental injury may also have been made by the family GP or a hospital casualty doctor, though neither of these is likely to make such a comprehensive recording of their findings. From the point of view of the local authority trying to establish its case, it is desirable for any injuries to be photographed, either by the police or hospital, as long as any photographs are of a high quality; the colour of bruising for instance can give an indication of when the injury occurred, but a poor photograph can be very misleading. Similarly, videotaped recordings of interviews with children have to be clearly visible and audible to be useful to the court.

If the child is referred to a paediatrician he may request a skeletal survey to try and detect old healed fractures, which if they have not been previously reported are another strong indicator of non-accidental abuse. He may do other tests to rule out a diagnosis of certain rare disorders which could be confused with non-accidental injury, as well as weighing and measuring the child, and observing his or her general physical and emotional development to see if it is age appropriate.

Doctors specialising in this field are becoming increasingly used to giving evidence, but they are in a delicate professional position. The vast majority of children brought to them *are* suffering from the results of accidents, and they need to be skilled in picking up 'messages' from the parents' behaviour in suspicious cases, as well as diagnosing the cause of the actual injury. If they question the parents too early or vigorously they run the risk that children needing treatment for whatever reason may not be brought at all if parents come to fear the consequences.

Further evidence and useful information about previous convictions may be provided by the police who may have questioned the parents (or others) with a view to a criminal prosecution. The police may be more skilled and experienced than other professionals in uncovering the truth behind a particular incident, but if their primary aim is to secure a conviction the child's welfare may be a secondary consideration. The guidance outlined in 'Working Together' emphasises a co-operative approach between police and Social Services, and this is becoming more widespread with the establishment of police teams specialising in child and family protection work. There remain some dilemmas, especially in the area of child sexual abuse where the prosecution of a suspected offender may rest on the child giving evidence, which could further exacerbate the original damage.

Child sexual abuse

On the subject of child sexual abuse, a solicitor may wonder if he should try and establish with the child if this really occurred. He should be aware that the child has already had to repeat her story to perhaps an initial confidante such as a teacher, then maybe a duty social worker, a doctor and a police officer. It would be an unwarranted intrusion for the solicitor or guardian to go over the same ground yet again, and would rarely be productive. The child needs to be aware that the solicitor and guardian know the content of her statement, and that if there is anything she wants to discuss further about it, she is able to do so. By the time the solicitor and guardian are involved, the child is more likely to need help with the consequences of her disclosure rather than the original events themselves. It is now accepted that most children *do* tell the truth, whether about sexual abuse or anything else, and the presumption should be to believe them in the absence of any contradictory evidence. The Criminal Justice Act 1991 covers the competence of children as witnesses (sections 52–55). Having scrutinised the evidence submitted by the other parties, the solicitor must weigh its significance, distinguish fact from opinion, and decide if any of it is inadmissible. It should be noted that section 41(11) allows the court to consider hearsay evidence arising from matters covered by the guardian's report, and section 96 relaxes the rules on children's unsworn evidence. In addition, the Admissibility of Hearsay Evidence Order 1991 abolished the hearsay rule in all family proceedings from 14 October 1991. Once an allegation of sexual abuse has been made, no family can resume its previous relationships unchanged, and the main task of the solicitor and guardian working with a child client in these circumstances is to help her make realistic choices for the future to promote her safety and self-esteem.

(b) The law

The guardian will rely on the child's solicitor for advice concerning all the legal options open to her in making the most appropriate recommendation to the court. As well as being thoroughly well versed in the Children Act and its accompanying Regulations and Court Rules, the solicitor should be aware of case law that could be relevant to the current matter. He may seek permission from the legal aid authorities to take counsel's opinion on a particularly complex point of law.

(c) Witnesses

The child's lawyer is unlikely to call many witnesses of his own, if the case being presented by the local authority has his support. He should know in advance who is to be called by the other parties, so that he can cover any gaps in the case. He may call the guardian to speak to her report or give evidence as an expert or to provide further information arising from her investigations. He may also call a witness who the guardian thinks has a particular contribution to make on behalf of a child, but who may have been overlooked by the local authority. This might be a relative or neighbour for instance. If the solicitor is calling an expert medical witness, he may seek the agreement of the court for him to attend at a stated time or to be on call to minimise the disruption to his clinical work.

The child as witness

The solicitor may decide to call the child himself, especially an older one who may be giving separate instructions. He has to weigh up the advantage to the child of having his view stated directly to the court, against how nerve-racking the experience might be for the child and what sort of witness he would be. He has a similar choice to make in advising the child whether or not to remain in the court room throughout the proceedings, or just to come in at the beginning and the end. If this is to happen, the solicitor or guardian should ensure that there is someone suitable to wait with the child, or arrange for him to be released so that he can return to school. Occasionally the child might decide to sit through the case, but then finds he is bored or upset, and the solicitor should check periodically that he still wants to be there. He should also use some discretion over what is desirable for the child to hear; it would not be in his best interests to hear about the instability of his parents' marriage or to learn that his brother was illegitimate for instance, and the solicitor should be prepared to ask the court to exclude the child if it becomes necessary to protect him from hearing sensitive information. Rule 16(2) covers such circumstances; the solicitor or guardian should explain to the child that information which is private to other people in the case is going to be dealt with, which is why he is being excluded from this part of the hearing.

(d) Disclosure of the reports

These considerations might also apply to sharing the various reports with the child client. A social worker or guardian should be prepared to justify everything they write in a report, but the need to furnish the court with all the details of the case can be at odds with the need to safeguard the interests of the child. I find it especially difficult to give an accurate description of the parent, who may be of very limited intelligence or have a criminal record, without debasing him in the eyes of his son or daughter. For this reason, I would prefer a paraphrase of the report to be shared with most children rather than the complete version. Again, the solicitor should use his discretion and it might be necessary in the case of an older child giving separate instructions to be completely open with what is being said in order for him to have the right of reply.

The disclosure of reports and other documents is primarily a task for the solicitor and ideally should be done at least seven days before the final hearing so that any inaccuracies can be challenged or corrected. He should ensure that whenever possible the child client understands the gist of why the matter has come to court, and what solution is being proposed, so that he can make his own wishes and feelings apparent. The solicitor has a duty to convey his child client's views to the court, even if he does not agree with them, in the same way that he would for an adult client, and the child needs to know this.

(e) Preparation of the child

The child, his parents and foster parents are all likely to be anxious about the final hearing, whether or not they are to attend. It is easy for lawyers who are so familiar with the court to underestimate its mystique and powerful aura for the average layman. In his final interview with the child, the solicitor should help the child to decide whether or not to attend court. An older child might find that attendance would be beneficial in helping him understand the reasons for his present situation, and the plans being made for his future. On the other hand, the prospect of going to court and being the centre of attention may present a considerable ordeal to the child, and he should not be persuaded against his wishes. When the child is excused attendance the solicitor should ensure that he is told the outcome promptly by someone who can explain what the decision means. If the child is to attend, the solicitor can help to put him at ease by showing him the empty court room, explaining who will sit where, introducing him to the usher and making sure he knows where the lavatory is. It is also helpful to suggest he brings something to do while he is waiting, and a young child could be kept occupied with the drawing material on pages 108–112.

In some circumstances the child might not want to come face to face with his parents or some other person present, and in that case the solicitor should try and arrange in advance for the child to wait somewhere separately. The clerk is usually sympathetic to this sort of problem—indeed one that I know is prepared to vacate her own office to allow the child to be comfortable. The magistrates are often prepared to see the child briefly outside the court, with a trusted person present, so that he may be released from further attendance and can go back to school. This is especially helpful in the case of very young children who quickly become fractious, or where the parents are distressed and angry and it is necessary to avoid the child becoming embroiled in a row.

The final hearing

On entering the court, the solicitor should ensure that the child, if present, is sitting next to a trusted person, either his parents if that is appropriate, or the guardian or someone else such as a foster mother or teacher (though permission may have to be sought in this case for a person without party status to be in attendance). The guardian will usually sit next to the child's solicitor, so that they may confer during the hearing; points may be raised in evidence that the guardian may wish the solicitor to query on her behalf, and he should always consult her before finishing the examination of a witness.

Order of witnesses

The normal sequence of events is for the local authority solicitor to present the case and then to call witnesses, followed by the parents' solicitor, with the child's solicitor following. Each party may cross-examine the evidence in turn, followed by the parents' and child's solicitors' closing speeches. The position of the child's solicitor as the last speaker is useful in that he can tidy up any matters that have not been properly covered previously. If the solicitor is taking separate instructions from the child, the guardian is likely to be unrepresented, but she has the right to be heard and to cross-examine witnesses, usually between the solicitor for the parents and the solicitor for the child. None of these rules need be rigidly applied, and the parties may agree with the court to a different order of presentation, perhaps to accommodate an expert witness, or to assist the court in understanding the issues at stake. Now that all parties can see the witness statements and reports in advance of the hearing, there is more scope for a negotiated agreement at the final stage. There may be some concessions that can be made between the solicitors with the agreement of their clients prior to the hearing, which are then presented to the court. Sometimes the negotiations take place outside the courtroom; some courts are prepared to delay sitting in order to facilitate agreement, while others may consider their judicial function is being undermined by this informal process.

As with all child care work, it is important for solicitors and guardians to use language that is comprehensible to the children and families involved without being patronising. The court hearing offers a unique opportunity for all concerned to examine the problems experienced by a family and to try and find a resolution that benefits the child, or at least minimises further damage. For parents it may be a painful experience to be publicly confronted with their shortcomings, but it may also be the first time they have really understood the problem, and why professionals are concerned for their child. This insight can be the first step towards change, which can benefit this child and perhaps prevent the removal of other children in the future. While it is important to prove the need for an order, care should be taken not to be unnecessarily destructive of parents, whose limited abilities need to be enhanced rather than further eroded. Very needy parents who cannot properly care for their children may still take comfort if it is acknowledged that they were not deliberately cruel to their child, or themselves faced so many difficulties that they could not act as the good parents they would like to have been. Apart from considerations of common humanity towards parents who are likely to be very distressed, it is important to realise that they will always be significant in some way to the child, even if the links have worn very thin at this particular time. Research shows that the majority of children in care do return home eventually, even if they are adults themselves before they can rebuild the relationship with their original family. (See *Patterns and Outcomes in Child Placement* (HMSO, 1991) for further information concerning the comparative success of placements within the extended family—see the recommended reading list on page 103.)

The solicitor acting on behalf of the child may not have a very active role to play at the final hearing if he is in basic agreement with the local authority. On occasions he might need to bolster up the local authority's case, perhaps by more vigorous cross-examination of the parents; the local authority solicitor may have been more restrained in the knowledge that the social worker has to preserve a working relationship with them. It may be sufficient to support what has already been said, or to clarify the details of the local authority plan such as the arrangements for contact or the financial support to be given to relatives caring for the child.

However, in a contested case, the solicitor might need to be far more pro-active in testing the evidence and using his advocacy skills on behalf of the child. The guardian's report will provide him with most of the material he needs, but he should be prepared to call the guardian or expert witnesses to support his case. Whether or not the child's solicitor contests the case, he has a vital role in keeping the child's interests at the forefront of the court's consideration. It is easy for the proceedings to degenerate into an argument over the rights and wrongs of particular events in the past, and for the court to lose sight of the principal issues concerning the child's future. The child's solicitor can ensure that attention is focused on the child's needs rather than disputes between the adult parties. He can use his advocacy skills to test the evidence of witnesses, to draw out the guardian's views, and to clearly state in his concluding address that the child's needs are paramount and how he believes they should be met.

After the hearing

When the court has made its decision the solicitor needs to conclude his work with the guardian and the child.

If the decision went against the guardian's recommendations, she may ask the advice of the solicitor about an appeal on behalf of the child, which is to the High Court but not any longer by way of a re-hearing. Appeals must be lodged within 21 days of the order. She should in any case ensure that the notes of her work are stored securely in case of an appeal, or if she is re-appointed in a subsequent discharge application.

To conclude his work with the child, the solicitor should ensure that he is told the outcome of the proceedings, and the local authority's plans if a Care Order is made, preferably by doing this himself if the child is old enough to understand, or by making sure that the social worker relays the decision quickly to the child if he is not at the court hearing in person. The solicitor may talk to him about an appeal if he is taking separate instructions. He should also say that children in care have their cases reviewed regularly when they should have the chance to express their concerns, and that there is a complaints procedure in operation (section 26) which the social worker should explain to the child. The child also has the right to come back to court for the discharge or variation of an order or to seek a variation of contact. The Children Act entitles the child to initiate proceedings but it is difficult to see how he could do so without adult help. The guardian's duties finish with the termination of the case, so it may be appropriate for the solicitor to be available to the child for future advice in this respect, and to make sure the child and his caretakers know how to contact him.

Criminal injuries compensation

If the child has suffered serious injuries, including sexual abuse, the solicitor may advise the person having parental responsibility for him, or the local authority if he is in care, to apply for compensation (even if there has been no criminal prosecution). Further information and an application form can be obtained from:

The Criminal Injuries Compensation Board
Blythswood House
200 West Regent Street
Glasgow G2 4SW

Conclusion

Representing children is a demanding but worthwhile undertaking, requiring a creative and flexible approach. With care and patience, and a willingness to go at the child's pace, the lawyer can guide and advise his young client, and obtain on his behalf the maximum benefit from the opportunities now available under the Children Act 1989.

Solicitors on the Law Society's Children Panel are sometimes isolated from other practitioners either through geographical distance or because they are the only specialist in their firm. To keep up to date with the many changes in this field it would be worthwhile to subscribe to one of the periodicals available, and to join a multi-disciplinary professional support group such as the BAAF* Legal Group, the local court users group, the Family Courts Services Committee if invited, or an informal group of child care solicitors, paediatricians, guardians and social workers which may meet locally to promote good practice and share information. The Law Society Legal Practice Directorate can put panel members in touch with existing regional groups of child care solicitors, and can supply a draft constitution and assistance in setting up a new group.

* Membership details can be obtained from:

British Agencies for Adoption and Fostering
11 Southwark Street
London SE1 1RD
Tel: 071–407 8800.

The Law Society's Family Law Committee's guidance for solicitors working with guardians ad litem

This guidance represents a revised version of that issued in May 1986 for use by solicitors involved in child care cases. Throughout this guidance references to 'the Act' or section numbers refer to the Children Act 1989 and sections of it, unless the contrary is shown. Equally, references to the Family Proceedings Courts (Children Act 1989) Rules 1991 (S.I. 1991 No. 1395 (L.17)) are denoted by FPCR appearing after the rule number and references to the Family Proceedings Rules 1991 (S.I. 1991 No. 1247 (L.20)) are denoted by FPR.

The Children Panel

The Children Panel covers 'All proceedings under the Children Act where there is provision to represent children'.

The emphasis is on the representation of children but members will also be available to represent other parties such as parents and grandparents, given their knowledge of the proceedings. Although the Act provides for children to become parties to 'private' law proceedings, with the leave of the court, it is likely that, at least at first, the vast majority of children requiring representation will be in child protection and care proceedings. However, given the way that the Act interprets 'public' and 'private' law proceedings, members should be competent to represent a child in any proceedings.

The panel will cover all proceedings where children will be parties in terms of private and public law orders. It will therefore be necessary for all child care practitioners to be familiar with the full range of orders.

It is not intended that the new panel will cover adoption or wardship.

Adoption is a relatively small area of work and wardship in the future will be available in a more restricted range of circumstances.

Representation for the child

The guardian ad litem in care proceedings

Appointment of the guardian ad litem

A guardian ad litem will be appointed by the court in proceedings specified in s.41(6) unless it is thought not to be necessary to do so to protect the child's interests (see also Rule 2 and 10 FPCR and Rule 4.2 and 4.10 FPR). It is estimated that guardians ad litem will be appointed in 90% of cases which in some areas represents a significant increase on the number of appointments prior to the Act's implementation.

A guardian ad litem will be chosen from local panels of experienced social workers. It is hoped that delays in appointing guardians ad litem under the Act will be minimised or avoided whenever possible (see Rule 10 FPCR and Rule 4.10 FPR). However, where a solicitor finds him or herself appointed to represent a child alone the solicitor should always enquire of the court if and when a guardian ad litem is to be appointed. If the court has no plans to appoint a guardian ad litem and the solicitor wants one to be appointed, the solicitor is entitled to apply for one to be appointed (See Rule 10 FPCR and Rule 4.10 FPR).

The guardian ad litem's role

The role of guardian ad litem has been extended by the Act. Guardians ad litem will be appointed earlier in the proceedings, their first duty being to appoint a solicitor for the child if one has not already been appointed. Guardians ad litem will no longer just give advice on whether or not the order applied for should be granted. A guardian ad litem may therefore be called upon to advise the court on matters such as:

- directions;

- the allocation and transfer of proceedings;

- any conditions that could or should be attached to orders, e.g. contact;

- interim orders;

- timetabling;

- where the child has sufficient understanding to refuse to consent to medical treatment;

- the menu of orders available to the court.

(For further details see s.41, Rule 11 FPCR and Rule 4.11 FPR.)

In view of this expanded role guardians are required to attend all the hearings in the case unless given leave not to do so (see Rule 11 FPCR and Rule 4.11 FPR). It is anticipated that the guardian's new role may mean that s/he will need greater assistance from the solicitor than previously on matters concerning the powers of the court and its proce-dures—particularly in view of the truncated timescales under the Act. Clearly, it will also be necessary for the solicitor to liaise closely with the guardian ad litem to ensure that provisional dates for hearings are convenient.

Guidance on what to do when a conflict of interest arises between the solicitor, guardian or child is set out below.

Appointment of solicitors

A child who is the subject of care proceedings under the Act is a party to those proceedings (see Rule 7 FPCR and Rule 4.7 FPR). In care proceedings under Parts IV and V of the Act a solicitor for the child can be appointed in three ways:

(i) by the child direct;

(ii) by the guardian ad litem (see s.41, Rule 11 FPCR and Rule 4.11 FPR);

(iii) by the court (see s.41).

A summary of the relevant provisions concerning legal aid and remuner-ation is set out at Annex A.

Panel members undertaking

Solicitors who are members of the Children Panel are bound by an undertaking in the following terms:

'I undertake that, when representing children in proceedings covered by the Children Act 1989:

1. Subject to paragraph 2, I will not normally delegate the preparation, supervision, conduct or presentation of the case, but will deal with it personally.

2. In each case I will consider whether it is in the best interests of the child to instruct another advocate in relation to the presentation or preparation of the case.

3. If it is in the best interests of the client, or necessary, to instruct another advocate:

   3.1 I will consider and advise the guardian ad litem (and the child if of appropriate age and understanding) who should be instructed in the best interests of the child.

   3.2 I will obtain an undertaking from that advocate to:

   (a) attend and conduct the matter personally unless an unavoidable professional engagement arises; and

   (b) take all reasonable steps to ensure that so far as reasonably practicable a conflicting professional engagement does not arise.'

The expectation is that panel members will conduct the advocacy in a case themselves. However, if it is in the best interests of the client or necessary to instruct another advocate panel members should first consider instructing another panel member. However, if it is appropriate to instruct counsel panel members may wish to instruct a member of the Family Law Bar Association. Details of the membership of this Association can be obtained from the Bar Council, Records Officer, 11 South Square, Grays Inn, London WC1R 5EZ (Tel: 071 242 0082). Where counsel is instructed s/he must meet both the solicitor and the child in advance of any court hearing to ensure that any preparation which is necessary following the conference can be done. However, conferences should be sufficiently close to the hearing to ensure that the child can appreciate the link between the conference and the court hearing. Consideration should be given to holding the conference at a neutral venue familiar to the child.

The solicitor who acts for the child

A solicitor instructed on behalf of the child has the child for his or her client but will obtain instructions from the guardian ad litem unless the solicitor believes it would be appropriate to take instructions from the child (see post).

In all cases the solicitor should see the child for whom s/he is acting and the solicitor should discuss with the guardian ad litem when and how it would be appropriate to see the child. This re-inforces the point made in the Report of the Inquiry into Child Abuse in Cleveland 1987 that 'the child is a person, not an object of concern'.

Where a solicitor is instructed prior to the appointment of the guardian ad litem s/he should not try to perform the roles of both solicitor and guardian ad litem. Rule 12 FPCR and Rule 4.12 FPR state that:

> 'A solicitor appointed under section 41(3) or in accordance with rule (4)11(2)A shall represent the child . . .
>
> (b)   where no guardian ad litem has been appointed for the child and the condition in section 41(4)(b) is satisfied, in accordance with instructions received from the child, or
>
> (c)   in default of instructions under (a) (instructions from the guardian ad litem) or (b) in furtherance of the best interests of the child.'

This will entail **gathering** together and **testing** as much information/ evidence as possible and (if possible) talking to the child and anyone else who might be able to provide relevant information or opinions. The relevant evidence should be presented to the court to assist the court in deciding what order, if any, it should make.

Where a guardian is subsequently appointed the solicitor should then take instructions from the guardian in the usual way—even where the guardian takes a different view from that formed by the solicitor about what is in the child's best interests. Such differences of opinion should, however, be discussed with the guardian.

The relationship between the solicitor and the guardian ad litem

The solicitor takes instructions from the guardian ad litem unless the child has sufficient understanding to instruct a solicitor personally and wishes to do so. This means that a solicitor should never express his or her personal opinions to the court. The relationship between the solicitor and the guardian ad litem should essentially be one of partnership building on the separate but complementary roles of the solicitor and guardian ad litem. Some guidance on this is given in preceding sections of this guidance. The fact that the roles are complementary should enable the solicitor and the guardian ad litem to agree a division of responsibilities at an early stage so as to ensure that no unnecessary duplication of functions takes place. Throughout the proceedings the solicitor and guardian ad litem should co-operate closely and be involved in continued consultation so that they can consider together how a case should be conducted and how they should respond to changing circumstances. In particular, the solicitor and guardian ad litem may need to consider together whether or not an appeal should be lodged. Section 42 sets out the rights of guardians ad litem to have access to local authority records. The solicitor and guardian ad litem will need to consider whether they should rely on the expert reports obtained by the local authority or whether reports from one or more independent experts should be obtained (see Annex A: legal aid).

Further guidance on the role of the guardian ad litem and the guardian's relationship with the solicitor is contained in:

(a) Rules of Court

(b) official guidance such as:

— the Manual of Practice Guidance for Guardians ad Litem and Reporting Officers;

— the Manual of Management for GALRO Panel Managers;

(c) National Association of Guardians ad Litem and Reporting Officers publications.

Interviewing children

A solicitor should be careful when interviewing any child not to raise issues in a way which could be potentially damaging and/or counter-productive. The solicitor and guardian should always be careful to try to elicit the child's true wishes and feelings—particularly where the child may be put under undue pressure to agree to a course of action which is acceptable to the other parties involved in the case. Further guidance on how to interview a child is set out in Annex B. It is important to make sure that a child understands the nature of a solicitor's duty of confidentiality and further guidance on the nature of that duty and how to explain its effects is set out in Annex C.

Where a guardian ad litem has been appointed s/he is also under a duty to explain matters of this nature to the child (see paragraph 11 of the National Association of Guardians Ad Litem and Reporting Officers' Code of Practice which states 'A guardian ad litem must ensure the child understands, in an age appropriate manner, the importance of the proceedings . . . the guardian ad litem should ensure the child is prepared for the court hearing'). If a guardian ad litem has been appointed the solicitor should therefore clarify whether the solicitor or guardian should carry out this function or whether they should do it jointly.

A child is like any other client to the extent that a solicitor must ensure that the client knows what is going on and what is likely to happen. A solicitor should not assume that any client will necessarily understand things like how a court works, what the court's processes are, who its personnel are, what the effect of different orders is and what the timescale of events is likely to be. This understanding certainly cannot be assumed when a child is the client and not only must the solicitor explain but s/he must explain in terms which the child will be able to understand. A simple and effective explanation of courts is contained in *Susie and The Wise Hedgehog Go To Court* by Madge Bray published by Hawksmere.

Attendance at court

It is the expectation that the panel member will personally attend all hearings in a particular case in the light of the personal undertaking. If this is not possible any agent of the solicitor should be well versed in all aspects of the case including being able to advise on convenient dates for future hearings.

The provisions relating to the courts' powers to direct that the child shall or shall not attend court are contained in s.95, Rule 16 FPCR and Rule 4.16 FPR. If there is no order, the solicitor should seek instructions from the guardian ad litem (or where appropriate the child) as to whether the child should attend court.

Conflicts of interest

(a) Between the child and other parties to the proceedings

It is clearly inappropriate for a solicitor to act for the child where s/he has been initially approached by a parent or any other party to the proceedings with whom the child's interests may or do conflict. It would also be inappropriate for the solicitor to act for the child where s/he had previously acted for another party to the proceedings, e.g. in the context of separation or divorce proceedings and in so doing had acquired relevant knowledge.

(b) Between two or more children

Where a solicitor is representing more than one child in the proceedings s/he must be equally aware of the possibility of a conflict arising. This issue is most likely to arise when the solicitor is receiving instructions direct from one or more of the children. The first question to determine therefore is whether or not one or more of the children is of sufficient understanding to instruct the solicitor direct (see below). If a solicitor finds him or herself with instructions from the guardian and/or one or more children, s/he must then consider the question of conflict. If there is a conflict of views the solicitor must carefully consider whether s/he can continue to act for any of the children involved in the light of the information s/he has received at that time. If the solicitor takes the view that s/he must cease acting for all or some of the children s/he should inform the guardian ad litem and the court of the position so that separate representation can be arranged for the children. The solicitor must not allow himself or herself to be swayed by the possibility that withdrawal might cause a child either to lose confidence in arrangements for his or her representation or to be disadvantaged by the involvement of a second new solicitor.

(c) Between the child and the guardian ad litem

Sometimes the child and the guardian ad litem will disagree over what would be the correct outcome of the case. In these circumstances a solicitor must always act on instructions and should never give his or her own views. It is the duty of the solicitor to act on the instructions of either the guardian ad litem or the child but a solicitor should only accept instructions from the child if the solicitor considers that the child is of sufficient understanding to give instructions. A solicitor's professional training is not well designed to equip him or her to make such an assessment unaided although solicitors who are members of the Children Panel will probably have undergone some training in child development or will have gained a certain amount of knowledge through experience. The solicitor should take account of the psychological state of the child and consider whether or not the child is functioning at his or her chronological age—although as is implicit in the word 'understanding' a child's age is only one factor in determining whether or not the child should give instructions.

In trying to assess a child's competence, the solicitor should meet the child; take into account the views of the guardian ad litem; seek assistance, for example, from the child's teachers, foster parents, etc., and where there is any doubt take professional advice from a child psychologist or child psychiatrist. Reference should also be made to the principles in *Gillick* v. *West Norfolk and Wisbech Area Health Authority and DHSS* [1986] A.C. 112, *Re R. (A Minor) (Wardship: Consent to Treatment)* [1991] 3 W.L.R. 592, *Re. J. (A Minor)* [1992] *The Times*, 15 July and *Re. H. (A Minor)* [1992] *The Times*, 5 June and further guidance contained in the Manual of Practice Guidance for Guardians ad Litem and Reporting Officers.

Where a solicitor decides s/he should take instructions from the child s/he should discuss the position with the guardian ad litem who has a duty to help the child instruct the solicitor personally (see paragraph 4.4 of the National Association of Guardians Ad Litem and Reporting Officers' Code of Ethics which states 'The child may be of an age and maturity to hold different views from the guardian ad litem about how her interest will best be served. The guardian ad litem must respect this, and ensure that an older child may see her solicitor alone'). When this situation arises the guardian ad litem's role continues (see Rule 11 FPCR and 4.11 FPR) and s/he can address the court direct. To assist the guardian ad litem in this, Rule 11 FPCR and 4.11 FPR provide that the guardian ad litem can ask the court for separate legal representation. Under the terms of the Civil Legal Aid (General) (Amendment) (No. 2) Regulations (S.I. 1991 No. 2036) guardians ad litem are not entitled to legal aid although under regulation 9 of the Guardian ad Litem and Reporting Officers (Panels) Regulations (S.I. 1991 No. 2051) the local authority is under a duty to meet any reasonable expenses incurred by guardians in respect of relevant proceedings.

If a child is giving instructions to the solicitor direct, it is important for the guardian ad litem and solicitor to ensure that this does not adversely affect the provision to the court of all the material relevant to the case. Any solicitor or guardian ad litem who faces difficulties over the performance of their duties is entitled to apply to the court for directions at any time (see Rule 11.9 FPCR, Rule 4.11(9) FPR, Rule 14 FPCR and Rule 4.14 FPR).

Any guardian ad litem or child who loses confidence in a solicitor is entitled to seek termination of the solicitor's retainer (see Rule 12 FPCR and Rule 4.12 FPR). Both the guardian ad litem (or child if appropriate) and solicitor can make representations if an application is made. The fact that the child is instructing the solicitor direct is not sufficient grounds for the guardian ad litem to seek the termination of a solicitor's retainer.

Expert witnesses

Any solicitor needing advice over the choice of an expert witness may obtain help from one of the organisations noted below. Solicitors taking instructions from the guardian ad litem should not find it necessary to ask an independent social worker for assistance. However, where the child's instructions conflict with those of the guardian ad litem, and the solicitor, therefore, acts on the child's instructions, solicitors needing assistance from an independent social worker may obtain help from fellow practitioners or one of the following organisations:

Local Support Groups (see Annex D)

Local Child Guidance Clinics

The Register of Independent Experts c/o 31 Woodstock Avenue, Ealing, London W13 9UQ (Tel: 081 579 9890)

Independent Representation for Children in Need (IRCHIN), The Bungalow, 23A Hawthorn Drive, Heswall, Wirral, Merseyside L61 6UP (Tel: 051 342 7852)

The Legal Practice Directorate Information Office, The Law Society, 50 Chancery Lane, London WC2A 1SX (Tel: 071 320 5710)

Solicitors should tell expert witnesses of the legal aid rates of payment which will apply (see regulation 60 of the Civil Legal Aid (General) Regulations 1989).

Solicitor who acts for a parent

Under the Legal Aid Act 1988 (Children Act 1989) Order 1991 (S.I. 1991 No. 1924) the means and merits tests will be waived where any parent involved in proceedings under s.31 and ss.43-45 applies for legal aid. Where an appeal against care proceedings is brought the means test (but not the merits test) will continue to be waived.

As in the earlier section on conflicts of interest, it would clearly be inappropriate for a solicitor who has been approached by or acted for a child in proceedings to then act for a parent. It would also be inappropriate where a solicitor is consulted by a parent prior to imminent proceedings, for the solicitor to interview the child. Solicitors will naturally also need to be alert to the possibility of conflicts of interest between parents.

If the solicitor and client disagree the general principle is the same as in other fields of law: solicitors advise and clients instruct. In child care cases, this means that the solicitor should advise the parent(s) that the court will be deciding the case in the child's best interests and therefore recommend a child centred approach. Nevertheless the solicitor must follow the parents' instructions and advocate their case in court—even if the solicitor personally believes that those instructions are not in the child's best interests.

The solicitor should also be aware of the style of advocacy expected in child care cases; although the advocate must be firm and assertive, a hostile or over-adversarial approach is likely to be counter-productive.

If a parent needs to consult an independent social worker/expert reference should be made to the organisations listed above.

Further assistance

Training courses

The Law Society approves training courses for solicitors joining the Children Panel. These deal specifically with the practical problems faced by solicitors representing children. Details are available from the Professional Standards and Development Directorate of the Law Society. The bibliography set out below may also provide useful background information.

Local child care support groups

See Annex D.

Bibliography of child care law

The Children Act.

The Family Proceedings Rules.

The Family Proceedings Courts (Children Act 1989) Rules 1991.

Clarke Hall and Morrison on Children, Butterworths, 10th ed., loose-leaf, 1985.

Guidance and Regulations on the Children Act produced by the Department of Health including the latest edition of 'Working Together'.

Hershman D., and McFarlane A. *Children: Law and Practice*, Jordans, looseleaf, 1989.

Children Panel newsletter

This is sent to all members of the Law Society's Children Panel.

ANNEX A

Legal aid

The child will be entitled to legal aid in the child's name and all applications for legal aid under the Act will be administered by the Legal Aid Board.

There are three routes for obtaining legal aid under the Act:

(i) in the normal way subject to the means and merits test;

(ii) pursuant to an emergency application;

(iii) if care and emergency proceedings are commenced under ss.31, 43 or 44 or an application is made under s.25, legal aid will be available for the child (and others: parents and those with parental responsibility) as of right irrespective of means and merits save that, in the case of applications under s.25, legal aid will only be available to the child on this basis.

The following regulations govern legal aid arrangements under the Act:

(a) The Legal Aid Act 1988 (Children Act 1989) Order 1991 (S.I. 1991 No. 1924);

(b) The Civil Legal Aid (General) (Amendment) (No. 2) Regulations 1991 (S.I. 1991 No. 2066);

(c) The Legal Aid in Criminal and Care Proceedings (General) (Amendment) (No. 2) Regulations 1991 (S.I. 1991 No. 1925).

Additional guidance on legal aid is contained in the Notes for Guidance on the Children Act which are inserted in the Legal Aid Handbook 1991. In general terms the provisions in the Civil Legal Aid (General) Regulations 1989 (as amended) concerning experts' reports and the Notes for Guidance in the Handbook still apply. This means that it is preferable to obtain prior authority from the Board before instructing an expert. Where leave of the court is necessary before obtaining an expert's report, the solicitor should be careful to ensure that the fact that leave has been obtained is drawn to the Board's attention, otherwise the grant of prior authority by the Board will be delayed. An estimate of the fee for the expert's report may also be of help to the Board.

Remuneration

The provisions relating to legal aid remuneration under the Act are contained in:

(a) The Family Proceedings (Costs) Rules 1991 (S.I. 1991 No.1832);

(b) The Legal Aid in Criminal and Care Proceedings (Costs) (Amendment) (No. 3) Regulations 1991 (S.I. 1991 No. 2037);

(c) The Legal Aid in Family Proceedings (Remuneration) Regulations 1991 (S.I. 1991 No.2038); and

(d) The Legal Aid in Family Proceedings (Remuneration) (Amendment) Regulations 1991 (S.I. 1991 No. 2112).

The Legal Aid in Family Proceedings (Remuneration) Regulations 1991 provide that an enhanced rate of remuneration may be payable where this is reasonable having regard to:

' (i) the exceptional competence with which the work was done, or

(ii) the exceptional expedition with which the work was done, or

(iii) any other exceptional circumstances of the case including, in the case of care proceedings, the fact that the solicitor was a member of the Law Society's Children Act panel' (sic).

ANNEX B

Interviewing children — principles and checklist

[This annex is taken from the Open University's *Children Act 1989: Putting it into Practice, Focus on Law* pack. It is reproduced with the kind permission of the Open University.]

There are three main principles to remember when talking to children:

1. Take time: the interview needs to be on the child's schedule and at the child's pace.

2. Take the child's thinking and language abilities into account: that is, do not use words and concepts that s/he is not familiar with or will not understand. Make sure you avoid technical terms.

3. Listen rather than talk.

Checklist

This stems from the idea that no one should ever go into an interview 'cold'.

- Do your research. Read all relevant reports — medical, social work and school. Make sure you know whether the child has been through other interviews and how productive they were. If it does not constitute a breach of professional ethics speak with other involved professionals, the parents, foster-parents and other relatives and close friends. If appropriate, explain your role to the parents. Try to find out something about the child on a personal level which may help you to break the ice.

- Do not keep the child waiting. Start the interview on time.

- Sit next to the child at a level comfortable for both of you — do not have your desk between you and the child.

- Begin by explaining what the interview is for. Say who you are and what your role is. Explain that it might be necessary for you to tell other people what has happened, but also say which people you do not have to tell.

- Gear the length of the interview to the age of the child: a maximum of half an hour (preferably less) for a child under five years old, 45 minutes for a child between the ages of five and eight, and an absolute maximum of an hour for a child over eight. However, be guided by how the child responds.

- Give the child enough time to answer your questions at his/her own speed. Leave a proper amount of time for the child to ask questions.

- Regularly check that the child understands what is being asked and said.

- Do not ask leading questions. Many abused children in particular may have learned to survive by anticipating what adults want to hear. Persistent questioning can also be counter-productive.

- If you are taking notes, explain why and be prepared to read them through with the child.

- Be willing to work in unusual ways. For example, a child may find it easier to draw a picture showing what happened.

- Assume the child is speaking the truth, while allowing for this assumption to be rebutted.

- Leave time at the end of the interview to tell the child what is going to happen next. Say what you are going to do, and why, and allow the child to comment on this proposal.

ANNEX C

Confidentiality and privilege—child abuse and abduction

[Taken from the Professional Standards Bulletin No. 5, July 1991.]

The following guidance has been produced by the Standards and Guidance Committee and the Family Law Committee and is a revised version of the guidance on confidentiality and privilege in cases of child abuse and abduction originally produced by the Family Law Committee in September 1987.

The guidance has been revised in the light of problems encountered by practitioners. Typically, the solicitor has either received information from a client or is about to receive information from a client, which he or she considers privileged, but which, if given to the court, police or social services, might protect the child or children at risk.

This guidance attempts to set out some general principles to which a practitioner should have regard and considers how these are affected depending on who is the client. The guidance gives examples of how certain situations might be dealt with as well as giving suggestions of bodies which may be able to give further help.

(A) General principles

1. The Committees take the view that child abduction is merely one example of child abuse and therefore any guidance given applies equally to cases of abuse and abduction.
2. A solicitor has two basic duties to a client whether parent or child: (a) the duty to act in the best interests of his or her client and (b) the duty of confidentiality.

(a) The duty to act in the client's best interests

Clearly the nature of this duty depends on who is the client. In considering the duty to act in the client's best interests the solicitor will need to draw a distinction between those children who are competent to give instructions and those who are not. A child who is competent to give instructions should be represented in accordance with those instructions. If a child is not competent to give instructions the solicitor should act in the child's best interests.

(b) The duty of confidentiality

A number of preliminary points can be made *before* considering how the situation is affected by the question of who is the client:

(i) Is the information confidential?

It has been held at common law that when communications are made by a client to his or her solicitor before the commission of a crime, for the purpose of being guided or helped in the commission of it, this constitutes a move outside the solicitor/client relationship and any communications made are not confidential and the solicitor is free to pass them on to a third party. The solicitor will therefore need to consider whether or not the proposed action is in fact a crime and reference should be made to the appropriate provisions e.g. the common law offence of kidnapping or the provisions of the Child Abduction Act 1984 and the Child Abduction and Custody Act 1985 and provisions relating to child abuse.

(ii) Assuming that the information received is confidential, which will usually be the case, a solicitor also has a duty to the court (as opposed to the client). As a result the solicitor may still be ordered by the court to disclose the information—for instance in a wardship case—see *Ramsbotham* v. *Senior* (1869) LR 8 Eq 575 (*Rayden and Jackson on Divorce and Family Matters*, para. 44.47 16th ed., 1991, Butterworths.) In all cases it is the solicitor's duty not to mislead the court. See Chapter 14 of *The Guide to the Professional Conduct of Solicitors*.

(iii) In circumstances other than those outlined above the Committees are in favour of the principle of absolute confidentiality being maintained save in truly exceptional circumstances. Any solicitor considering the disclosure of confidential information should bear in mind that he or she is bound by a duty of confidentiality and may only be entitled to depart from this duty in exceptional circumstances.

In considering what might constitute exceptional circumstances a solicitor must consider what would be in the public interest. There is a public interest in maintaining the duty of confidentiality. Without this the public interest in being able to confide in professional advisers would be harmed and the duty of confidentiality would be brought into disrepute. There is also a public interest in protecting children at risk from serious harm. Only in cases where the solicitor believes that the public interest in protecting children at risk outweighs the public interest in maintaining the duty of confidentiality does the solicitor have a discretion to disclose confidential information.

It may be that a parallel can be drawn with the case of *W* v. *Egdell* [1990] 1 All ER 835. In this case a consultant psychologist felt obliged to reveal his report showing that W, if released from a secure hospital, was likely to commit further murders. It was held that although the duty of confidentiality should rarely be breached it is sometimes essential for a balancing act to be carried out to determine whether greater public interest lies in revealing the information or in maintaining the duty of confidentiality. A similar test was applied in In *re. M* [1990] 20 Fam Law 259.

(iv) If a solicitor, having considered the arguments set out above, feels that he or she may be entitled to disclose confidential information he or she should, in addition, consider the following points:

(a) Is there any other way of remedying the situation other than revealing the information? If so, thought should be given as to whether this course would have the desired effect of protecting the child and if so whether it should be taken.

(b) If the information is or is not disclosed will the solicitor involved be able to justify his or her actions if called upon to do so by the court or Solicitors Complaints Bureau? Before revealing any information a junior solicitor or member of the solicitor's staff should always consult with his or her principal on the appropriate course of action to take.

(B) Who is the client?

Five different situations have been considered.

(i) An adult

(a) An adult (parent or otherwise) who is not an abuser but is asserting that a third party is abusing a child.

In this situation a solicitor's duty to act in the best interests of his client might entail suggesting that the client alerts a relevant agency—e.g. police or Social Services Department him or herself or accepting instructions to do so. If the client does not wish to alert a relevant agency or does not give the solicitor instructions to do so the solicitor must accept the client's decision and may remain bound by the duty of confidentiality. A solicitor in this position should explain the legal position and can seek to persuade the client to disclose the abuse or allow the solicitor to do so. If the client refuses to follow either of these courses of action the solicitor may still exercise his or her discretion and reveal the information. This will only be the case if the public interest in revealing the information outweighs that of keeping it confidential.

(b) An adult who is abusing or the solicitor believes will abuse a child.

Where the client is an abuser or potential abuser it becomes necessary to consider not only the duty to act in the client's best interests and the duty of confidentiality but also whether or not any distinction should be made between continuing and future abuse and how and when a solicitor should explain his duty of confidentiality and any possible limitations to it.

Where a client is continuing to commit an offence or is proposing to commit an offence, the duty to act in the client's best interests means that a solicitor should explain the legal implications of what a client has done, is doing or is proposing to do. For example, a client who tells a solicitor that he has or is proposing to abduct a child should be told about the common law offence of kidnapping, the provisions of the Child Abduction Act 1984, the Child Abduction and Custody Act 1985 and the client's duty to obey orders of the court, if there are any which are relevant. Similar steps should be taken in relation to cases of child abuse.

In the case of future abuse if, after receiving the solicitor's advice on the legal position, the client is dissuaded from his criminal course of action the solicitor's duty of confidentiality is absolute. In the case of a continuing offence, which as a result of the advice then ceases, this is equally the case.

In the case of a continuing crime which does not cease as a result of the advice given, or a future crime which the solicitor understands from the client may or will take place, the solicitor must then go on to consider whether or not it is justifiable to breach his or her duty of confidentiality bearing in mind the guidance set out above. See A.2.(b)(i) and (iii). In addition it may be appropriate for the solicitor to point out that he or she has a discretion to inform a third party of the offence that is being, may or will be committed.

(c)   An adult who has been abused or is being abused.

As above, where the client is an adult who has been or is being abused the duty to act in the client's best interests would entail outlining the legal position and suggesting where the client, or the solicitor on the client's behalf, could go for help. A solicitor in these circumstances is absolutely bound by the duty of confidentiality to the client but it is always permissible to try to persuade the client to reveal the abuse.

(ii) A child who is being abused

The extent of a solicitor's potential entitlement to breach the duty of confidentiality will depend on whether the child is mature or immature. It will often be difficult for a solicitor to judge the maturity of a child and the solicitor will need to make a judgement on the basis of the child's understanding. Reference should be made to the principles in *Gillick* v. *West Norfolk and Wisbech Area Health Authority and the DHSS* [1986] A.C. 112 and the Children Act 1989. In difficult cases it may be appropriate for a solicitor to approach a third party with knowledge of the child and expertise in this area, for instance, the guardian ad litem involved in the case (if any). A solicitor should never breach the duty of confidentiality unless he or she strongly suspects or knows that abuse has, is or will take place.

(d)   A mature child who is being abused.

Where a mature child is the client the guidance in (c) above applies except that a solicitor may have a discretion to breach the duty of confidentiality where he or she knows or strongly suspects that younger siblings are being abused or where the child is in fear of his or her life or of serious injury.

(e)   An immature child who is being abused.

Where an immature child is the client the solicitor's duty is as in (c) above in relation to doing the best for the client. A solicitor can try to persuade the client to reveal the abuse. If the client refuses the solicitor is not absolutely bound by the duty of confidentiality and may feel, bearing the above arguments in mind, that he or she is entitled to disclose what the child has told him or her to a third party. This should only be done if it is in the public interest and there is no other less oppressive method of dealing with the situation (such as a guardian ad litem disclosing the abuse—see example 3 below).

Where the client is an immature child the solicitor may need to consider whether or not he or she should reveal any disclosures to the child's parents. It may be that a disclosure of information to another third party such as the police or social services would best serve the interests of the client.

(C)   The decision to disclose and possible consequences

Any client whether child or adult has a right to be made aware of when and in what circumstances the solicitor's duty of confidentiality may be breached. The decision of when and how to tell the client of the solicitor's decision will clearly be a difficult one although it is thought to be preferable to make the position clear during the first interview. This will present the solicitor with a dilemma—if he or she fails to disclose the abuse he or she will not be in a position to help protect the child from further abuse. On the other hand, if the solicitor tells the child he or she may breach the duty of confidentiality there is a risk that further disclosures will not be forthcoming from the child. Despite this if a solicitor is about to breach his or her duty of confidentiality there is a high expectation that the solicitor will tell the client of his or her decision and explore with the client how this should be done. However, in the end it is for the solicitor to exercise his or her professional judgement about when and how to explain the duty of confidentiality to any client; it is impossible to formulate a rule that can be applied in all circumstances.

Any solicitor who tells the client that the solicitor will breach the duty of confidentiality should inform the client that the client is entitled to terminate the solicitor's retainer if such disclosure is contrary to the client's wishes. However, it is almost inevitable that the breaching of the duty of confidentiality by the solicitor will cause the client to terminate the solicitor's retainer whether or not the client is informed by the solicitor of his or her intentions. Upon the termination of the retainer the duty of confidentiality still remains, subject to the solicitor being able to justify a breach of the duty in the exceptional circumstances referred to in section A.2. (b)(iii).

(D) Working examples

The illustrative examples given below set out four situations in which a solicitor needs to consider whether or not her duty of confidentiality should be breached.

Jane Potter is a solicitor in private practice. She does general family work and some criminal law work. She has four matters where she is concerned that the children involved may be at risk of harm. She does not know who to tell, or whether indeed she can tell anyone of her concerns. These are her problems and the advice that was given her by Professional Ethics and the Legal Adviser's Branch of the Law Society.

1. Jane is acting for the mother of a child who has recently been made a ward of court. After becoming a ward of court the child continued to reside with the mother. Accommodation for the mother and child is in itself a cause for concern, being a hostel for homeless persons. The rest of the accommodation is shared with a number of other adults. The mother has come to see Jane and tells her that the child is subject to abuse by another adult in the house. The mother does not want this information to be made known to anyone else as she is fearful that the child will be taken away, particularly as the child is already a ward of court.

    Jane is under a duty of confidentiality to her client which means that any information given to her cannot be passed onto another without the consent of the client. Jane should strongly advise the client to reveal the abuse and discuss with the client the options that are open to her of expressing her concerns to social services and seeking alternative accommodation; of social services encouraging the local authority to remove the alleged abuser from the hostel; and of reporting her suspicions to the police.

    Jane is in the very difficult position of having to decide whether her duty of confidentiality towards the mother is outweighed by the public interest in the reporting of the abuse. Jane must explore very carefully the basis of the mother's allegations to be satisfied that they are true. She must also explore the nature of the abuse to the child. Jane should look at the terms of any order made in the wardship proceedings to see if there are any matters which must by order be reported to the court. It is for Jane to decide on all the evidence whether there is a strong case for believing that the child will suffer serious abuse such as will outweigh her duty of confidentiality towards her client.

2. Jane is acting for a young man who is charged in the local magistrates' court of an offence of indecent assault upon a young child. The client has admitted the offence to Jane, and in the course of interview has indicated to Jane that he has committed more offences than the police know about. The client however is on bail, one condition being that he should not contact the child in question. One evening after working late Jane popped into the local McDonalds and saw her client seated at a table with the child. There was no other adult present. Jane did not know what to do and left the building.

    Jane is not under any duty to inform the police of the breach of the bail conditions. No one is under any duty to report a suspicion of an offence. However Jane must advise her client of the effect of his breaching his conditions of bail. She should seek to persuade her client not to repeat this breach. If there is no real evidence that the client was abusing the child, Jane should take no further action. If the client indicates to her that a further offence has taken place, Jane must try to assess whether there is a substantial risk of the child suffering significant harm in future from the client. If so, Jane may inform a third party and cease to act for her client if she is satisfied there is no other less oppressive way of dealing with the situation. If Jane believes that there is no serious risk of harm to the child, but the client indicates that he will continue to see the child, she is not under any duty to inform a third party of the breach. This case is difficult as the solicitor has the very onerous task of trying to establish whether the client is telling the truth or not. If the solicitor had evidence to suggest that the client was positively misleading her then it may be that she would have to cease acting because the solicitor client relationship had broken down.

3. Jane is also acting in care proceedings for a boy aged 12. The child has not been attending school and has been involved in solvent abuse. No guardian ad litem has been appointed to date. The child is living at home with his mother and his mother's boyfriend. Jane has seen the child on his own in order to ascertain if the child is

old enough to give proper instructions and has decided that he is. In the course of the interview the child stated that the mother's boyfriend has sexually abused him on a number of occasions. The child is adamant that Jane should not reveal this allegation to anyone as he does not wish his mother to know.

Jane's discussions with the local authority reveal that the local authority intend that the child remain at home after a care order is made, as the local authority wish to 'work with the family'.

Jane should urge the local court to appoint a guardian ad litem as soon as possible. With the help of the guardian ad litem Jane must try to assess the truth of the allegations made by the child. If the allegations are well founded the guardian ad litem would be able to reveal them as a guardian ad litem is an officer of the court and is not bound by a duty of confidentiality to the boy in the same way that Jane is. If the court refuses to appoint a guardian ad litem, Jane must decide what to do by reference to the principles set out earlier in this guidance. This is equally the case where a guardian ad litem is appointed but the child does not reveal the abuse to him or her—indeed the fact that the child does not reveal the abuse to the guardian ad litem may be a factor for Jane to consider in deciding how serious the abuse is and whether or not it should be revealed.

4. Jane's final problem is in a matrimonial case where she acts for the mother. The father has obtained a residence order in respect of the child. Jane has advised her client fully on the effect of the order in relation to removing the child from the UK. Nevertheless her client has disappeared with the child and both are assumed to be out of the jurisdiction. Jane has received a telephone call from her client indicating that she wishes Jane to continue to act for her. Jane should of course advise her client to return to the jurisdiction and to return the child. Jane is not under any obligation to reveal the client's whereabouts, if she knows them, unless or until she is ordered to do so by the court. If there is no prospect of Jane being paid for continuing to act for the client, she can end the retainer. She is certainly under a duty to inform the legal aid authorities of her client's action; though not of her whereabouts, if her client is in receipt of a legal aid certificate.

Two weeks later Jane receives news that her client and the child are destitute, living on the proceeds of begging in the streets and sleeping rough. Jane is concerned that the child, who is three years old, could be in danger.

Jane is under no obligation to reveal the client's whereabouts. She must strongly advise her client to return to the jurisdiction for the sake of the child. If Jane is satisfied that the child is in serious danger she may breach her normal duty of confidentiality towards her client by making disclosure to the court of her client's whereabouts.

(E) Bodies to contact

Child abduction

Official Solicitor's Department, 81 Chancery Lane, London WC2A 1DD, telephone 071 911 7127/7045/7047.

[The Lord Chancellor's Department is the 'Central Authority' in relation to the Hague and European Conventions.]

The Foreign and Commonwealth Office, Consular Department, Clive House, Petty France, London SW1H 9HD, telephone 071 270 3000.

The Passport Department, Home Office, Clive House, Petty France, London SW1H 9HD, telephone 071 271 8629.

'Reunite' National Council for Abducted Children, P.O. Box 158, London N4 1AU, telephone 071 404 8356.

The Police.

Child abuse

The Police.

The Local Authority Social Services Department.

The Children's Legal Centre, 20 Compton Terrace, London N1 2NU, telephone 071 359 9392.

NSPCC, 67 Saffron Hill, London EC1, telephone 071 242 1626.

Criminal Injuries Compensation Board, Whittington House, 19 Alfred Place, London WC1E 7EA, telephone 071 355 6800.

Criminal Injuries Compensation Board, Blythswood House, 200 West Regent Street, Glasgow G2 45W, telephone 041 221 0945.

ANNEX D

The Children Panel Support Groups Organsisers

BEDFORDSHIRE

Gareth Woodfine & Partners
Exchange Building
16 Cuthberts
Bedford MK40 3JB

DX: 5619 BEDFORD

Telephone: (0234) 270600

BERKSHIRE
(see Buckinghamshire)

BUCKINGHAMSHIRE
(covers Berks, Bucks & Oxon)

Mary Ann Edwards
Winter-Taylors
Park House
London Road
High Wycombe
Bucks HP11 1BZ

DX: 4403 High Wycombe

Telephone: (0494) 450171

DEVON

Kay Butterfield
Michelmore Davies & Bellamy
Harston
Church Street
Sidmouth
Devon EX10 8LT

DX 48704 SIDMOUTH

Telephone: (0395) 512515

DORSET

Richard Byrne
Lester Aldridge
Russell House
Oxford Road
Bournemouth
Dorset BH8 8EX

DX 7623 BOURNEMOUTH

Telephone (0202) 786161

ESSEX

Bruce M Edgington
Simpson Robertson & Edgington
'Barringtons'
Hockley Road
Rayleigh
Essex SS6 8EH

DX 50604 RAYLEIGH

Telephone: (0268) 778311

GREATER MANCHESTER

Iain Hamilton
Child Concern
Walls Johnston & Co
19 Market Place
Stockport
Cheshire SK1 1HA

DX 19657 STOCKPORT

Telephone: (061) 480 3431

HUMBERSIDE

Margaret Lloyd-Jones
Forum for the
Representation of Children
Graham & Rosen
8 Parliament Street
Hull HU1 2BB

DX 11925 HULL

Telephone: (0482) 23123

Kenneth W Wood
Beverley & Wood
99 Mary Street
Scunthorpe
South Humberside DN15 6LA

DX 14703 SCUNTHORPE

Telephone: (0724) 841758

LANCASHIRE

Shirley Pollard
Marsh & Co
22 Sun Street
Lancaster LA1 1ER

Telephone: (0524) 68102

Miss Angela Nield
Fentons
32 High Street
Oldham OL1 1JA

Telephone: (061) 652 4125

LINCOLNSHIRE

S P G Fisher
Thimbleby Fisher
Lindum House
10 Queen Street
Spilsby
Lincs PE23 5JE

DX 27951 SPILSBY

Telephone: (0790) 52219

LONDON

Ann Aitken
Offenbach & Co
60 Great Marlborough Street
London W1V 2BA

DX: 42723 Oxford Circus North

Telephone: (071) 491 1343

Charlotte Collier
Atkins Hope
78 North End
Croydon
Surrey CR9 1SD

DX: 2629 Croydon

Telephone: (081) 680 5018

NOTTINGHAMSHIRE

Tony Priest
Rotheras
2 Kayes Walk
Stoney Street
The Lace Market
Nottingham NG1 1PZ

DX: 10028 NOTTINGHAM

Telephone: (0602 414415)

OXFORDSHIRE
(see Buckinghamshire)

SHROPSHIRE

Philip Kenny
R Gwynne & Sons
Edgbaston House
Walker Street, PO Box 23
Wellington
Telford TF1 1HF

DX: 23107 TELFORD

Telephone: (0952 641651)

TYNE AND WEAR

Barry Speker
Samuel Phillips & Co
86 Pilgrim Street
Newcastle Upon Tyne
NE1 6SR

DX: 61028 NEWCASTLE
UPON TYNE

Telephone: (091) 232 8451

WEST MIDLANDS

Ceila Grew
Grew Wilson & Co
25 Warwick Row
Coventry CV1 1EY

Telephone: (0203) 633377

Ian Young
Young & Lee
432 Stratford Road
Sparkhill
Birmingham B11 4AD

DX: 13017 BIRMINGHAM

Telephone: (021) 772 5012

WEST YORKSHIRE

Stephen Butler
Representatives of Children
in Civil Courts
Messrs Stephen Butler
3rd Floor Sunbridge Chambers
13 Sunbridge Road
Bradford
Yorkshire BD1 2AY

DX: 11738 BRADFORD

Telephone: (0274) 391461

WILTSHIRE

Nicholas Beach
Goughs
30 Market Place
Devizes
Wiltshire SN10 1JG

DX: 42904 DEVIZES

Telephone: (0381) 726913

WORCESTER

Jonathan Brew
Harrison Clark
5 Deansway
Worcester WR1 2JG

DX: 716260 WORCESTER

Telephone: (0905) 612001

WALES

Roger Edwards
Roger Edwards & Co
22 Commercial Street
Tredgar
Gwent NP2 3DH

Telephone: (049525) 2865

Reading list

General

Department of Health. *Children Act 1989 guidance and regulations: volume 1: court orders*, HMSO, 1991.

Department of Health. *Children Act 1989 guidance and regulations: volume 7: guardians ad litem and other court related issues*, HMSO, 1991.

Current social work

Department of Health. *Patterns and outcomes in child placement: messages from current research and their implications*, HMSO, 1991.

Department of Health. *Protecting children: a guide for social workers undertaking a comprehensive assessment*, HMSO, 1988.

Department of Health. *Working together under the Children Act 1989: a guide to arrangements for inter-agency co-operation for the protection of children from abuse*, HMSO, 1991.

Seminal

Adcock, Margaret and White, Richard. *Good-enough parenting: a framework for assessment*, British Agencies for Adoption and Fostering (BAAF), 1985.

Blom-Cooper, Louis. *Child in trust: the report of the panel of enquiry into the circumstances surrounding the death of Jasmine Beckford*, London Borough of Brent, 1985.

Lord Justice Butler-Sloss. *Report of the inquiry into child abuse in Cleveland 1987*, HMSO, 1988 (CM 412.).

Guardians ad litem

Clark, Don. *Representing children: child interviews: a pictorial aid for guardians ad litem and Child Care Panel solicitors*, Kent and Sussex Independent Counselling Agency Publications, 1989.

Monro, Pat and Forrester, Lis. *The guardian ad litem*, Jordans, 1991.

National Association of Guardians ad Litem and Reporting Officers. *Code of ethics for guardians ad litem and reporting officers: code of practice for guardians ad litem and reporting officers: role and function of panel managers*, NAGALRO, 1991.

Timms, Judith. *Manual of practice guidance for guardians ad litem and reporting officers*, HMSO, 1992.

Child care law

Bainham, Andrew. *Children—the new law*, Jordans, 1990.

Clarke Hall and Morrison on Children. Consulting editor: Brenda Hoggett, 10th ed., Butterworths, 1985–, looseleaf, 2 vols.

Feldman, Linda. *Child protection law*, Longman, 1992.

Hershman, David and McFarlane, Andrew. *Children: law and practice*, Jordans, 1991–, looseleaf, 2 vols.

Open University. *Children Act reference pack*, 1991. *Children Act focus on law pack*, 1991. *Children Act trainers' pack*, 1991.

Spencer, John and Flin, Rhona. *The evidence of children: the law and the psychology*, Blackstone, 1990.

The Law Society. *The enforcement of English maintenance orders abroad – a guide for solicitors.* 1992.

White, Richard *et al. A guide to the Children Act 1989*, Butterworths, 1990.

Practice

Dawson, Peter and Stevens, Robert. *Family proceedings court: a handbook on the Children Act 1989 and the rules for practitioners and others*, Barry Rose, 1991.

King, Philip and Young, Ian. *The child as client*, Jordans.

Lord Chancellor's Department. *Children Act 1989: court user guide*, HMSO, 1991.

Mallender, Paul and Rayson, Jane. *How to make applications in the family proceedings court: a step by step guide to the Children Act in the magistrates' court*, Blackstone, 1992.

Forthcoming

Burrows, David and Williams, Richard. *Ascertainable wishes of the child*, Jordans, Jan. 1993.

The family court practice. Editor-in-Chief: The Hon. Mrs Justice Bracewell, Jordans, Dec. 1992.

Family law directory. Edited by Elizabeth Walsh, Jordans, Dec. 1992.

Periodicals

Adoption and Fostering. British Agencies for Adoption and Fostering (BAAF), 1977–. Quarterly. Articles on social work, medical and legal issues concerning children.

Childright. Children's Legal Centre. Monthly. Wide-ranging and informative articles on topical legal issues to do with children.

Family Law. Jordans, 1971–. Monthly. Includes child care law reports.

Family Law Reports. Jordans, 1980–.

Panel News. Independent Representation for Children in Need (Irchin). Quarterly. For guardians and child care solicitors.

Practitioners' Child Law Bulletin. Longman, 1989–. Ten issues per year.

Seen and Heard. National Association of Guardians and Reporting Officers (NAGALRO). Bi-monthly.

Tolley's Journal of Child Law. Tolley, 1989–. Quarterly.

Notes on the illustrations

The drawings are intended for photocopying for use in work with children—they would benefit from enlargement first.

1. The house provides a useful jumping off point for getting the child to talk about himself. You may need several copies if there are several places to describe such as his own home, a children's home, a divorced parent's home or foster home. The people can be represented by stick drawings or just face outlines and names—don't forget the family pets!

2. The information sheet is to be filled in with the correct names, addresses and telephone numbers and given to the child or his caretakers. This will help him remember who you are, the nature of your job and how he can contact you.

3. The drawing of the court can be adapted to more closely resemble the real thing, or used as an introduction to what the child should expect.

4. The newspaper format could be used at a point when the child is ready to talk more freely about himself. Some of the information could be light-hearted, such as favourite pop groups, food or colour. You could then lead on to the child's understanding of past events and what he wants to happen in the future.

5. The balloon can be simply used for colouring in as a diversion while waiting at court, or to occupy the child while you're talking about other things. You could also use it to lead the child into a discussion about the people he would most like to have with him for an adventure, and those (on the ground) he would leave behind.

Where I live

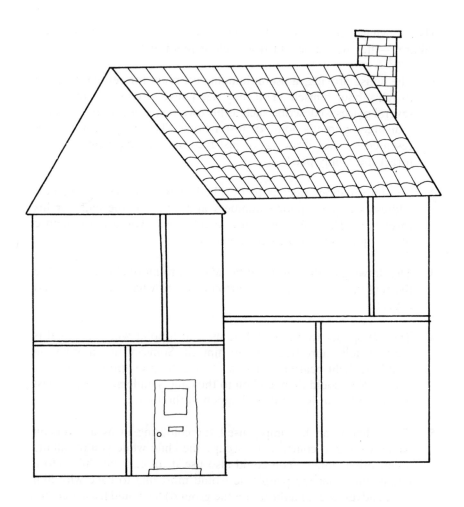

My solicitor is called _____

_____ will tell the people at

Court what I want to say to them.

My guardian ad litem is called _____

_____ will tell the people at

Court what would be best for me.

_____ is at:

_____ is at:

This is what the Court may look like....

This is all about me!

THE NEWS ABOUT

. . . .

Did you know that....?

WHAT A STORY!

Let's look forward to....

Back at the beginning....